ADDICTED TO PROGRESS

LEADING YOURSELF TO SUCCESS STARTS WITH IMPLEMENTING THE BASIC CONCEPTS OF SUCCESSFUL LEADERSHIP

BLAIR WILLIAMSON

Copyright

All rights reserved. Without limiting the rights under copyright reserved above, no part of this publication may be reproduced, stored in or introduced into a database and retrieval system or transmitted in any form or any means (electronic, mechanical, photocopying, recording or otherwise) without the prior written permission of both the owner of copyright and the publishers.

The people, events and information contained within this Book are strictly for educational purposes. If you wish to apply ideas contained in this Book, you are taking full responsibility for your actions. This publication is designed to provide accurate and authoritative information regarding the subject matter covered. It is sold with the understanding that the author and the publisher are not engaged in rendering legal, accounting, or other professional services. If you require legal advice or other expert assistance, you should seek the services of a competent professional.

Disclaimer: The author makes no guarantees to the results you'll achieve by reading this book. All business requires risk and hard work. The results and client case studies presented in this book represent results achieved working directly with the author. Your results may vary when undertaking any new business venture or marketing strategy.

Copyright @ 2024 Blair Williamson
First published 2024 Christine Robinson Global
ISBN: 9798339024651
Cover by Christine Robinson

DEDICATION

This book is dedicated to my amazing family, Corie, James, and Harper. You are my "why". You motivate me to be my best version. I love you with all my heart.

I lost my father, J.B. Williamson, on February 19, 2022, while I was in the middle of writing this book. My dad was my best friend for 44 years. He was my hero. My idol. He was the greatest father I could have asked for and the best grandfather my kids could have ever wanted. Family was first - always. I will miss him for the rest of my life. I love you Dad.

CONTENTS

Addicted To Progress i
About The Author ii
Introduction v

CHAPTERS

1 Full Commitment. 1
2 Good Leadership Is Key 7
3 First, Your Why. 19
4 What Is A Leader?. 24
5 Organization Under Bad Leadership 31
6 Leading By Example 36
7 Surround Yourself With Likeminded People. 39
8 "Let Them". 44
9 Comparing Yourself To Others 46
10 Patience Is A Virtue 49
11 The Power Of Confidence 51
12 Leaders Are Decisive 54

13	Public Speaking	57
14	Setting Goals	62
15	Make Good Choices	69
16	Holding Yourself Accountable	71
17	Continue Learning	73
18	Barriers: Relentless Progress	76
19	Be A Completer	84
20	Keep Your Social Media Clean	86
21	Work Just A Little Bit Harder	88
22	Consistency	91
23	The Art Of Successful Networking	97
24	Soft Skills - The Basics	102
25	Diversity	112
26	Building Your Team	116
27	The Importance Of Culture	129
28	What Is Progress?	135
29	Become A Mentor	137
30	Final Thoughts	141
	Glossary	146

ADDICTED TO PROGRESS

Congratulations for taking action to enhance your life by mastering the art of successful leadership! With this book, you will learn how to lead like a pro and create success for yourself by breaking down barriers and building a dynamic, motivated team. We will define your success and set you on a path to reach your goals. Being a productive leader is crucial in moving up the corporate ladder, taking your team to the next sales level, or taking your business to levels of success you have only dreamed about. You will learn how to confidently lead your team, your family, and your employees by motivating them to be the best they can be. You can immediately take the information in this book and implement it into your life. It doesn't matter what level of employee or business owner you are; you will start seeing positive results immediately! This book will explain the "how to"; it's up to you to do the rest!

"The surest way not to fail is to determine to succeed."

Richard Brinsley Sheridan

ABOUT THE AUTHOR

Blair Williamson has over a decade of experience developing training programs for entry-level employees, management teams, and everyone in between. He is an author, workforce development professional, entrepreneur, investor, nonprofit director, and public speaker. He believes that learning how to lead can be taught at a very young age and challenges parents to start educating and molding their children to become successful leaders while still in elementary.

"Respect, good communication, and making good choices are all part of being a good leader. Children can learn these traits as early as 5 or 6 years old. It is never too early to teach them how to be successful adults," says Blair.

Blair is originally from Texas and has lived abroad, working in several different countries in the Middle East. He has a unique perspective on the various methods used by successful people. He believes there is never one way to do things correctly, but there are common characteristics and techniques used by truly successful people that he will share throughout this book.

Blair has overcome several setbacks, failures, and knockdowns throughout his career. He believes these build character, strength, and patience, which are key to reaching your full potential. Where one might see a barrier or an obstacle, Blair sees it as a challenge. "So-called 'barriers' gets me excited! Others may think it's a good reason to try something else, quit, or go a different route. Not me, I'm going through it! I call it Relentless Progression!" says Blair.

Blair has had the chance to work for and work with multiple companies in various capacities throughout his career. He has built a solid reputation in his industry and an extensive network of business colleagues, mentors, and friends. Those experiences led him to entrepreneurial endeavors, where he became a successful business owner and investor. Blair's true passion is inspiring and motivating people from around the world and all walks of life. He believes each person can reach their own level of success if given the right tools to succeed. His brand's backbone is teaching people how to succeed and motivating them to reach their full potential. He teaches that being a solid leader is the core foundation that success is built on. He firmly believes that if you implement the information in this book in your everyday life, you will undoubtedly see positive results.

INTRODUCTION

I grew up in southeast Texas, in the small town of La Porte. It's tucked away between the bright lights of Houston and the salty waters of Galveston Bay. My father was the municipal court judge in La Porte for 32 years and an attorney for over 50 years. My mom was a legal secretary and office manager most of her life, then decided to work in the Middle East for a government contractor in 2003 at the start of the war with Iraq, in which she became extremely successful. This led to me working in the Middle East for several years. She has also published her own book about her experience in the Middle East and has always been a great writer. It's where my passion for writing came from.

My childhood was pretty simple for the most part. My parents split before I can remember but they remained friends throughout the years. From other people's perspectives, I'm sure it seemed I was spoiled, a little on the conceited side, and loud and obnoxious most of the time - definitely a class clown. We moved a lot but typically stayed within the La Porte city limits. My dad was married several times, and my mom was married three. So, although they loved me very much and were both extremely active and engaged in my upbringing, they didn't give me a good example of maintaining a healthy relationship, which has always been one of my many downfalls.

I played little league football, basketball, and baseball just like the majority of everyone else in La Porte. My dad helped coach most of my teams and my mom was my biggest fan.

I always looked back and thought I had a great childhood. To me, my parents were perfect, and I wouldn't have changed a thing.

Although I made decent grades and excelled in most sports, I wasn't pushed very hard to be great or to give it all I had. I was never held accountable really for anything that I was doing. Even though my parents were very active in everything I did, It was a very hands-off parenting approach when it came to accountability. It took me a long time to grow up. It is definitely different from how I raise my children, which has inspired me to write this book and to get involved with the kids in my local community as much as possible to ensure they have the resources, information, and tools they need to succeed.

INTRODUCTION

I eventually graduated college from Texas State University in San Marcos, TX, at the age of 34, and have had a pretty successful career since then. I've spent the majority of my career in the industrial construction arena, supporting the chemical plants and refineries in Southeast Houston.

The one thing I've always done well was observation. I would watch people who I deemed successful from an early age and would steal some of their characteristics, mannerisms, and traits. I learned very early by watching my parents, and other adults that I looked up to, that networking was very important. It's one of the things that I've always been good at, but nobody ever taught me that it was necessary. It was almost a wasted talent. But as I got older, I realized that I did it probably better than anyone I knew. Most people reading this probably think networking is easy; it's just talking to people, attending events, or it's just playing golf. That couldn't be further from the truth. Successful networking is an art. Turning those contacts you meet into business ventures, partners, or job opportunities is not something everyone is capable of. So, I was able to use that to my advantage. We will dive deeper into networking later in the book.

Observation became crucial to my later successes. I watched people at all levels. I looked at how they acted in different situations. I watched people fail miserably and learned valuable lessons from their mistakes. I watched people overcome obstacles and learned how to navigate through my own. I watched people speak in front of hundreds of people and learned how to keep a room full of people engaged. I watched leaders of organizations lose respect from their direct reports and were never able to gain it back. I learned that observation was important to my own success. I learned that if I just watched and listened, I would learn. So, that's what I did. And after years of observations and finally sitting down to interview and question leaders who I respected, I realized that the more successful individuals, although they may seem different on the outside, were actually very similar. They all had very similar habits and routines.

I've taken those experiences and I've laid them out in this book. I've made it simple to follow and understand. I've broken out the sections into smaller sections so it's easy to reference. This book will require you to think, do some written exercises, and use your brain a little, but it's to hold yourself accountable. It's to push you. It's to bring out some honesty and do some self-reflection. This book is about leadership and success. They go hand in hand. To be truly successful, you need to learn how to be a good leader. Good leadership is the most basic core fundamental of all successful business owners, entrepreneurs, and corporate executives. I will say this time after time during this book, success doesn't happen overnight. Patience. Steady progress is the goal. Steady progress equals success. Let's get into it.

SNAPSHOT

Have you ever truly given life your best effort? I don't mean in a certain situation or a moment in time. I'm referring to life in general. Have you dug deep and really tried to succeed in every aspect of your life? Most of us haven't. Most of us give minimal effort to meet certain criteria to maintain average and maybe progress every now and then. Most people are ok with that. Most people are completely satisfied with being among the average. An average job, an average house, an average car, average vacations, just average. I'd be willing to bet you are not one of those. I'd be willing to bet that since you picked up this book and started reading it, you want more.

Maybe you want more and don't know how to get there ...
Maybe you want more but need some motivation ...
Maybe you have reached a level in your career and are unsure how to reach that next level ...

This book will explore all those questions and require you to dig deep inside yourself and not only want more but will challenge you to get more. This book can bring the best out in you if you truly work through the process. We will pinpoint what is holding you back from reaching your next level. We will help you identify habits that may be detrimental to your success and give you some good practices to implement in your life. This book will lay out the ingredients for success and a plan of action for you to start improving your life immediately.

The waiting is over. You don't want to look back in 10 years and realize you are in the same place emotionally, financially, and physically that you are in this very second. You will be pushed to step outside of your comfort zone to really challenge yourself. You will be given tools to use daily that will increase your chances of becoming an absolute success story.

It doesn't matter your age, your gender, your ethnicity, your geographical location, or your upbringing. You are in the situation you are in because you haven't figured out how to change it. It's time to hold yourself accountable and commit to being truly successful. Once you remove the garbage from your thought process and commit to making no more excuses, then you will be open to new ideas and new beginnings. Your success is going to start with you getting your mind right. We will discuss some ways to help alleviate negative and unproductive thinking and start you on a positive path to reimagining your status in this world. Your true success starts now.

1

FULL COMMITMENT

For any process to have a truly positive outcome, you must be committed to that process. Commitment is simply a pledge or promise. You make commitments every day of your life. You make commitments to other people, such as family, friends, and coworkers. But when was the last time you made a real commitment to yourself? When was the last time you put your needs in front of those you care about? When was the last time you said no to a loved one? What you don't realize is that by putting other people first, you are sabotaging your own happiness, your own joy, and your own success.

What would happen if you committed to putting yourself before anyone? Do you think it would hurt those other relationships? Or do you think by ensuring your happiness and satisfaction first, you would be better equipped to help others in a whole different way? Most people think that by putting others first, you are doing them a favor. When, in reality, if you put yourself first, you would be able to help and support them even better. As we start to age and get older, we start compromising and settling for average. We give up on our dreams and goals and start trying to help others reach theirs. Why? When you were a child, you dreamed of big dreams. We all did. Nobody said to themselves when they were young, that when they get older, they want to be average. No child ever says that they want to be mediocre. When we were kids, we dreamed of being professional athletes, lawyers, doctors, business owners, etc. Why do we start settling as we age? Somewhere, as we begin to get older, we lose those dreams. We lose that spark, that motivation, that faith that we can do it. We start making excuses and start being "realistic". That's complete bullshit.

> ... we start compromising and settling for average.

What's realistic is that we are not being true to ourselves. We aren't putting ourselves in first place anymore. We start to lose ambition and start settling for less. And once you start the "settling" process, that sets the tone for the rest of your life. You start settling at work, you start settling with your health, you start settling with your relationships, and before you know it, your life is a big compromise. You've compromised your happiness and success by helping others reach theirs. This is not ok.

What you must do from this very moment on is to commit to yourself that you are going to put yourself before anything else in your life. You need to commit to excellence, not average. Commitment takes practice, focus, discipline, and hard work, but is well worth it. Once you make this commitment to yourself, you will start seeing positive changes in other areas of your life. You will start gaining a newfound respect from others. It will completely enhance your life on so many levels that you will wonder why you didn't do this earlier. Put yourself first. This doesn't mean treat others with disrespect or ignore their feelings, but in order for you to be truly supportive and give all you can to other relationships, you must take care of your needs first. Most people don't realize that you are actually hurting those other relationships by being committed to others before yourself. Those other people will eventually thank you and respect you for it.

Have you ever been on a flight and listened to the stewardess while they are going over the safety procedures before takeoff? They tell you in case of an emergency, the oxygen masks will drop from overhead. They always tell you to put yours on first, before helping others. You can't help anyone else if you can't breathe. This is the same process you should be implementing in all areas of your life, not just in emergencies.

This commitment that I am asking you to make is going to be hard. This is going to be different than anything you've done up until this point. But before we start digging into the actual processes and methods of success, you have to make a commitment to yourself right now. You have to promise yourself that no matter what, you will take care of YOU first.

In order to make your new commitment an actual habit, we need to practice. The more we practice, the more chances it will become a routine and spill over into your daily lives. Have you ever looked in a mirror and just talked to yourself? I seem to do this a lot. Not just in front of a mirror, but when I'm driving, cooking, working out, trying to go to sleep at night, and anywhere else you can think of. It actually helps me figure out different situations or obstacles I may be facing. One of the things you need to get used to is telling yourself you are committed to yourself. Say it to yourself enough that you believe it. Say it over and over. You are your #1 priority. And if you need to, get in front of a mirror, look at yourself in the eyes, and commit by saying, "I am committed to MY success". Look at yourself and remind yourself that "I am doing this for you". You cannot expect to help anyone else until you are truly committed to yourself. The more you say it, the more you believe it, and the more you will start acting like it.

Once you've made that commitment, you cannot break it. If you start to get sidetracked or deviate from your path, then go to a mirror and recommit. You must truly be committed to you and your success. Some days this will be harder than others, but eventually this will become your daily routine and you won't even reconsider going back to your old ways. Committing to yourself to do whatever it takes to be successful is how you must live each day of your life.

We will get into discussions later in this book about getting sidetracked and dealing with obstacles, but if you remain committed each day, you will be able to work through whatever life throws at you.

> "Most people fail, not because of lack of desire, but because of lack of commitment."
>
> Vince Lombardi

COMMITMENT CONTRACT

<u>Commit to yourself</u>: The mirror exercise and reminding yourself that you are your #1 priority is important and doesn't need to be taken lightly. But to even more fully commit to yourself let's take it a step further. We now know that to be truly successful in anything in your life, you must be committed to the process. So, for the sake of this book, and you taking action to grow yourself, it is extremely important that you stay committed to your actions to achieve the level of success you are seeking.

Too many times people have great ideas, important ideas, and ideas that could change their lives in a positive way forever, but there is no follow through. There is no true commitment to the process. Great things take time to cultivate. Do not expect yourself to reach your dreams and goals overnight. Commitment is key. Set your goals, but more importantly, make a commitment to yourself that you will stick with the process until your goals are achieved.

As you read through this book and start implementing it into your daily routines, stay committed. Do not do it half-ass, do it with the throttle wide open and full steam ahead.

Be committed to your own success because <u>nobody else will.</u>

Do you promise yourself to commit to your own success?
Do you promise yourself that you will do your very best each day to ensure that you are closer to your big goals than you were yesterday?

Sign on the line below if you are committed to your own success. This is a legally binding contract between you today, and you tomorrow.

Sign:

Date:

2
GOOD LEADERSHIP IS KEY

A strong, well-rounded leader is the core foundation upon which success is built. You won't see many truly successful people who are not strong leaders. Leadership is a learned behavior. Yes, some people are born with better leadership traits, but good leadership skills can be taught to anyone. Those that dedicate themselves to being an effective leader tend to get better results within their teams and organizations. Being a good leader means that you can motivate and inspire a group of people to reach their full potential. Good leaders can get more out of a group in a work environment than those who just maintain a leadership role within an organization. People can tell if you are a good leader or not. You cannot fake it. Being able to lead a group of people to work together and accomplish goals is crucial to becoming successful. You will undoubtedly rely on team members or coworkers to help you reach your goals. You need to know how to help inspire those individuals and create passion amongst them.

After studying dozens of successful leaders throughout the last several years, it's obvious that there are some common characteristics and behaviors among them. Work ethics, good communication, confidence, focus, and good decision-making skills are among the traits that these leaders each possess and set them apart from the crowd. We will dive into each of these characteristics throughout this book. These leaders do NOT make excuses or complain about things not going their way. They are problem solvers and laser focused. They are committed to being successful and ensuring their organization, business, or team is successful as well.

When you think about a leader you admire, what are their traits and characteristics? I'm sure you have seen or witnessed a person in a leadership role who does not lead effectively. I'm sure you've wondered how that person got into that role. This, unfortunately, happens quite often. People are put into situations without the proper tools or training to be effective. These people may have been great employees in a different role, but when you put them in a leadership role where they are responsible for motivating and inspiring others, they fail. Just because someone is educated in their craft and is extremely knowledgeable in their area of expertise, does not necessarily mean they should be responsible for a team, a department, or even a company. If those people do not seek proper advice or training, they will either fail miserably, or stay right there in that position, whatever that may be, without any further advancement.

There was a study in the 1960s that explained situations similar to this. Being promoted until you are unable to meet the requirements of the job by lacking the required skills and/or knowledge, is referred to as the Peter Principle. The Peter Principle, in short, states that a person will be promoted until he/she reaches a position in which they are incompetent. Then, they will stay in that position, achieving no more promotions. The Peter Principle suggests that this is inevitable for everyone. Eventually, you will be incompetent at a level in the hierarchy. Although an interesting study, I've always thought that people who think this way are small minded. They don't think big enough. I don't think that Richard Branson, Elon Musk, or Jeff Bezos ever let the Peter Principle hold them back. When you hit a "ceiling" at work, that is the time to dig down and start self-improving. Don't let others put limitations on your success. There are people who reach a level and are happy and content at that level and don't desire any further advancement, so they stay right there. As long as they are successful in that position and are happy with their achievements, then there should be no reason to force them to a higher level.

Believe me, I've witnessed my fair share of bad leaders in the workplace. I've seen an entire company culture obliterated due to the executive team at a company I was employed by. It was actually a sad place to work. The only people who could not see how bad the situation was, were the people creating the bad situation. It's a tough spot to be in when you are directly under lousy leadership. But it's an opportunity to learn and grow. You have to learn how to survive and thrive even in those situations. But I am going to teach you how to avoid being one of those "bad" leaders in this book, and how to handle situations where you might have to deal with difficult individuals in your workplace.

Good leadership is vital to any organization's success. And the higher up on the hierarchy those leaders are, the more responsibility they have in creating a company culture that promotes positivity and creativity, all while holding employees accountable. Leaders who lead other leaders have the most important role in the company. They must use their experience and influence to guide those leaders under their responsibility to ensure they are aligning themselves and their teams with the company's mission, goals, and values. A break in the chain at this level could cause a serious ripple effect that will negatively impact every group and individual under that person's scope of influence.

Being a good leader, constantly honing your leadership skills, and learning from other people's mistakes and successes will help you keep moving up the food chain. Be great at your current role. Even if you are in a job you're not happy with, be freaking awesome at it. Be so good that they don't have an option but to keep promoting you. This goes for business owners and entrepreneurs as well. No matter what you are doing for money right now, be the best at it.

Good leaders tend to continue to educate themselves throughout their life. They stay ahead of the game and work on improving their skills constantly. And, if you are leading a group of individuals, a company, or your own business, and your employees or team members are witnessing you continue to seek education and training for yourself, those individuals will likely end up following your lead. They will see you as a good example of someone continuing to better themselves and will want the same for themselves. Developing your leadership skills should never end. Becoming a better leader, a better person, a better team member, a better employee, a better boss, a better friend, should always be your top priority. Strive to be better.

Before we dive into the different sections in this book, I think it's essential that we get a pulse of your thoughts and ideas as of right now. I'm going to have you do some "prework", and later, after you've read the different sections, you can look back on this prework and see if your thoughts have changed any. Hopefully, this book will inspire you to challenge yourself to look at things a little differently. Have an open mind while reading, be honest while doing the work, and maybe you will learn how to do some of the things you are currently doing a little better, or maybe it's a good idea to stop some of the things you are doing and implement some of the other things you will learn instead. Either way, be open to change. Be open to learning and admitting to yourself that there are areas in your life where you could improve upon. Take your time and work on this pre-work before reading any further. This is part of the process.

> "If your actions inspire others to dream more, learn more, do more, and become more, you are a leader."
>
> John Quincy Adams

PRE-WORK – TAKE YOUR TIME AND FILL THIS PORTION OUT BEFORE MOVING FORWARD WITH THE SECTIONS

What is your definition of a leader?

List three leaders that you admire.

1.
2.
3.

What do these people have in common?

What are three characteristics of those leaders that you admire?

1.
2.
3.

Do you consider yourself a leader?

Yes: _____

No: _____

What is your best quality as a leader?

Where do you see yourslef in 5 years, and how do you plan to get there?

What is your definition of success?

Are you willing to commit to your own success?

Yes: _____   No: _____

Are you willing to put forth the maximum effort required with no excuses?

Yes: _____   No: _____

Do you currently have a mentor? If so, who is it?

Do you currently mentor anyone? If so, who?

What is the last course you've taken, seminar you've attended, book you've read, or educational podcast you have listened to?

What was the last networking event you attended?

What was the last networking success you had? (New client, business partner, career opportunity, etc.)

What is the biggest goal you have for yourself in life? Be honest.

What is the biggest goal you have for yourself this year?

What are you willing to sacrifice to reach your goals?

Do the people you surround yourself with support you on your journey to success?

Yes: _____   No: _____

Do you have people in your life that are holding you back?

Yes: _____   No: _____

Who are the top 5 people in your life that you are around the most during a normal week? This can be anyone (coworkers, friends, children, parents, etc).

1.
2.
3.
4.
5.

What would you say is your biggest "failure" in life?

Did you learn any lessons from that "failure"?

Are you comfortable speaking in front of a crowd? What is the biggest crowd you have spoken to?

What is your greatest fear?

On a scale of 1 – 10, 10 being the best, what is your confidence level of yourself professionally? Circle your answer.

      1   2   3   4   5   6   7   8   9   10

Do you consider yourself a good employee?

Yes: _____   No: _____

Do you participate, volunteer, donate, etc. to any charities or nonprofit organizations?

Yes: _____   No: _____

Who is the best boss you have ever worked for? And why?

What social media accounts do you use for your business and / or professionally?

If a potential client or employer were to look at your social media accounts today, do you think it would hurt your chances of working with them?

Yes: _____   No: _____

When you think about the progress you've made in your career over the past 5 years, are you happy?

Yes: _____   No: _____

What is your reason for wanting more out of your career or business?

Do you think your family and/or friends are proud of your success so far?

Yes: _____   No: _____

If you could change one choice you have made in the past 10 years regarding your career, what would it be?

3

FIRST, YOUR WHY

Some things in life are so important that nothing else matters unless those things are taken care of first. For me, it is simple: family over everything. That is my "why". Family is extremely important to me. I want my core group of people in my life to be safe, happy, and healthy. For them to remain safe, happy, and healthy, they must have a roof over their head, food in their bodies, access to good doctors, and live with as little stress as possible. I must ensure that I succeed in my career, so my family does not go without necessities. I take on the stress of providing so they can focus on achieving greatness in their own lives. It is my duty.

To me, success and taking care of my family are in the same sentence. Without my success, they do not have that security of being taken care of. They depend on me, and I take that extremely seriously. That is my driving force behind everything I do. When I feel tired, anxious, or stressed, I dig down deep and *do it for my family.* When I want to quit and give up, I dig down deep and *do it for my family.* When I want to sleep in, cancel a meeting, or not answer that phone call, I get my ass up, dig down deep, and *do it for my family.*

Do not get me wrong, I am human. Some days, I do not feel like getting out of bed at all. Some days, I wonder if I am making the right choices and start to stress about decisions I have made the day before. But one thing is exactly the same in every day of my life; I sit up in bed, put my feet on the ground, make no excuses, and start moving forward with Relentless Progression. This is how I live every single day of my life. Seven days a week, 365 days a year. Yes, I take vacations, and I take time out of each day to spend with my family without work interfering, but to me, it is all part of the equation of being successful.

My definition of being truly successful is providing for my family the best I can and raising my children to the best of my abilities. I want to be a solid role model for my son and daughter. I want them to look at me for inspiration, motivation, and hopefully be proud that I am their dad. I try to have as balanced a life as possible, but my family understands that dad must work to ensure we are all safe, happy, and healthy.

The term "safe, happy, and healthy" is a term I use in my prayers each day as I am getting ready to walk out of the door to take on the world. I ask God to please keep my family safe, happy, and healthy. But I understand that does not magically happen, I still must do my part. I believe in God, but I am not a big organized-religion type of guy. I believe that spirituality is a personal endeavor, I believe in prayer, and I believe that God gives you opportunities to succeed. I do not believe God chooses those who will succeed and who will not, but that he gives each of us opportunities to advance and puts us in situations where we are given choices to make. It is up to us to seize those opportunities and make good choices to ensure our personal growth and advancement.

Whether you believe in a higher being or higher purpose is up to you. My belief in my God has given me comfort, guided me when I felt lost, and pushed me through some tough situations when I was at my lowest points in life. As I have grown, I have leaned more and more on my spirituality to keep me calm and patient during stressful times. I understand that things will not always go my way, and I try not to lose focus on my end game as I navigate through short-term disappointments and setbacks. The goal is to keep moving forward. How ever you do that is up to you. Just make sure you are doing it. Steady progress is success. We will dive deeper into that very topic later in this book.

You must keep an open mind and be willing to put in the hard work. Success is not easy. If it were, everyone would be successful. Success is there for those that want it and do something about it. As I discussed earlier in the book, when you were a child, you didn't dream of being average. You wanted to be something great. You had big dreams, and you did not have any doubt that you could make those dreams come true. Why does it change over time? Allow yourself to dream, make those dreams your goals, buckle in, push the pedal to the floorboard, and just do it!

Identify your 'why'. Make that the sole reason you get up and get after it day in and day out. When you want to give up, think about your why. Your why should be enough to always push you forward.

First, Your Why. Work Page

What is your "why"?

What makes this your "why"?

What makes having a "why" so important?

Addicted To Progress ... Leading Yourself To Success

4

WHAT IS A LEADER?

We've established that good leadership is extremely important to be truly successful. But what is your definition of a leader? If you look up the word online, you will come up with several different variations, but they relatively have the same translation. A leader is someone who can influence a group or team of people to work towards a common goal. Given that definition, can you think of someone in your life who is a leader? It could be your boss, your coworker, your team captain, or your mom or dad. Leaders typically have different styles of leadership but are all striving for the same results. Being a good leader is being able to motivate and inspire people not only by words, but also by actions.

Are you a leader? The answer is simple: yes, you are. The real question is, are you a good leader? If you aren't, why aren't you? Do people respect you? Have you built a good team? Do you lead by example? Do you communicate well? These are things we will talk about throughout this book. Some people are born with leadership traits and abilities, but others can develop them with hard work and experience. Either way, we can all improve our leadership skills. It is an ongoing effort to become a successful leader.

There is no right or perfect way to lead, but most tend to fall into one of three different categories. Kurt Lewin, a psychologist, determined there were three basic leadership styles: Authoritarian, Participative, and Delegative style. Since his research in 1939, several more styles have been identified through other research by other experts. I think of the newer styles as sub-styles. Each person can still fit into one or more of the first three categories.

Authoritarian leaders tend to dictate policy and procedure and direct work to be done by the group without looking for any meaningful input. These leaders tend to "micromanage" and supervise their group very closely.

Participative leaders engage their group members in decisions and for input. They make their team feel important which creates commitment and typically higher quality work.

Delegative leaders are very hands-off. They offer little to no guidance to their group and leave decision-making up to them. These leaders will provide the necessary tools and resources, but power is basically handed over to the group.

Do you tend to fall into one of those categories? More than one? That's ok. There is no right way to lead. And from my research I've noticed that most leaders have a combination of traits and ways of handling different situations. It would be hard to put them just in one category.

I fall into more of the Participative Leadership style. I like to engage my teams and keep them involved in decisions. I believe this promotes creativity, sparks new ideas, and makes your team feel important. I live by this simple rule – Create inspiration & motivation, by collaboration. Not all group settings will allow this type of leadership, but it has worked for me for a long time. I do my best not to micromanage anyone. I've been in situations where I've witnessed people being micromanaged by their superiors. It creates an unhealthy work environment, in my opinion. And if you micromanage your employees, you are either not leading them correctly, or you do not have the right team members in your organization.

Leaders I admire all have a high level of drive and determination. They lead with confidence. They do not complain about problems, they look for solutions. They are team players and make others feel important. They tend to "grind in the shadows" without drawing attention to the hard work they are putting in. There is no need to brag when you are great, your success will be enough proof that you have made it.

The best way to learn is to listen, observe, and practice. I've watched and observed so many different people lead groups, teams, meetings, and entire organizations. I look at their mannerisms, their communication styles, their gestures, their engagements with their team members, their motivational techniques, and how they critique. Each person is unique. Some closely resemble each other, but none are just alike. By watching others, you will pick up on tidbits you can incorporate into your leadership style. You will also see things others do that you want to avoid.

Observe and watch how teams react to their leader. Are they engaged? Are they bored or unamused? Do they gossip about their boss? Do you feel they respect their leader? You can learn a lot by just observing. Put yourself in that leader's situation. What would you do differently?

I want you to walk away from this book with more confidence and a better understanding of what it takes to be a great leader. It's not easy. It takes years of tweaking your style to become a successful leader. It takes mistakes. It takes digging yourself out of tricky situations. But this is part of the learning process. The more experience you have at leadership, the better you will get.

> *"A leader is one who knows the way,*
> *goes the way, and shows the way."*
>
> **John C Maxwell**

Leadership is not something you turn on and off. You are either a leader or you aren't. Your team will look to you for advice and guidance. You need to be prepared to handle different situations and different people with different attitudes.

Leaders create a culture around them. Their attitude and work ethic spread throughout their group and organization. Be that inspiration that you would want out of a leader. As you read through these next sections, think of ways you can start to implement some of this information into your daily routines. Start small. But stay consistent. The more you implement, the more you practice, the better you will become.

What Is A Leader? Work Page

It is important to learn how to observe, talk with, and study leaders you admire. Read the directions below and see what you learn, you may be surprised.

1. Identify a leader who inspires you. This can be someone at work or in your private life, even a family member.
2. Schedule a minimum 1-hour block of time to sit with that individual and discuss leadership and what it means to them. Here are a few example questions to consider while speaking with them.
   a. What is their definition of a leader?
   b. What kind of traits do they think a good leader should possess?
   c. What kind of leadership traits do they possess?
   d. What kind of leadership style out of the three choices in the leadership section do you think this person mostly identifies with? Are they more than one style?
   e. Ask this person who they admire as a leader and why?
   f. Does this person have a mentor?
   g. Did this person start off as a good leader? Or did they have to work and tweak their leadership style to become successful?
3. Write in the space provided below anything that you learned from this individual that you may not have known before. Having conversations like this with people you admire or deem successful will help you understand what it takes to get to that level. Ask the questions and do a lot of listening.

Addicted To Progress ... Leading Yourself To Success

5
WHAT HAPPENS TO AN ORGANIZATION UNDER BAD LEADERSHIP?

Let's talk about what happens to a company or an organization under poor leadership. I want to get this out of the way early in the book so you understand how important it is to work hard at being a good leader. In my corporate career I've been fortunate enough to work in many different departments, in many different capacities, which has given me the chance to see how businesses are run from different angles. I've worked in Human Resources, Training, Workforce Development, Logistics, and Operations. I've also owned several companies and a franchise. I've even worked for a nonprofit. So, I've seen different types of organizations, from big corporations with over 40,000 employees to small businesses with as little as 5 employees, and how they are managed. I feel this has given me a unique perspective.

In my earlier days I worked for a government contractor overseas in the Middle East. Although I had some great experiences there and had some great leaders and mentors, I did have one person at one point who was my boss (I can't even give him the respect of calling him a leader) who made everyone's life a living hell. He was one of those guys that let you know several times throughout the day that he was in charge, and he was the "big dog" (other words and variations were typically used). His lack of leadership abilities and oversized ego were ultimately his downfall, but during his reign he made my life and others very unnecessarily difficult. My position was "Site Manager". I was young, probably 28 years old, but I already had a lot of leadership and management experience. He didn't like anyone else to feel like they had any control over any situation whatsoever, even if it was their responsibility. So, the stress of accomplishing my goals and daily tasks were multiplied by not having the right support and not having control over my areas of responsibilities. I eventually left, and eventually, he was terminated. And he was ultimately arrested on Federal charges and went to prison for stealing money from the company. So, not only was he a terrible leader, but he was also a criminal and extremely unethical.

Later in my career, I was a manager for a company in the Houston area where I had another "bad leader(s) experience". This was the worst company culture I had ever witnessed. Several leaders in this organization had no business being in the position they were in. They created a toxic atmosphere where most of the people who worked there, at every level, were miserable. I worked directly with these leaders, and the lack of support and knowledge they had left a lot of us feeling like we were on an island. They didn't understand their business, the people who worked for them, the departments they were overseeing, or how to lead. They didn't trust themselves enough to make decisions, so they questioned their experts' opinions and decisions, which made the experts frustrated and tired. The leaders, once again, were driven by ego. Everyone around them could see it, but for some reason, they couldn't. The only option the good employees had was to leave.

These two situations are fairly extreme. But in both situations the same result happened. The good employees ended up frustrated, unmotivated, became silent, and eventually left. The attrition rate goes through the roof. But the bad employees usually end up staying. They stay for the paycheck. They stay because they've got it easy and don't mind a bad leader because they typically have no ambition to be "better" themselves. So, the company ends up with bad employees being led by bad leaders. And I can tell you that exact thing happened in both of these situations. Good employees will not stick around and put up with bad leadership. They know they deserve better, and when the opportunity arises, they will leave.

Leadership starts at the top. Bad leadership trickles down to every nook and cranny in the organization. It leaves no stone unturned. It affects everyone. And eventually, the business will fail right along with the leadership. Don't be one of these statistics. Have more respect for yourself. And when you encounter a bad leader you can do one of two things - you can try to weather the storm and see if things get better, maybe try to move departments under a different supervisor, or you can look for a better opportunity elsewhere. I've chosen the second option in both situations. Although I stayed in both situations for a good period of time (in the second situation over two years). But eventually I was able to find a better opportunity and leave on my terms. And I can tell you this, the day I left, the moment I walked out of the door for the last time, I felt immediately better. Like the world was lifted off of my shoulders. Bad leaders can make your life very difficult. And even if you try not to, it's hard not to bring that stress and anxiety home each day, especially if you are trying to do good at work and the leader is sabotaging your progress. So, the lesson here is that leadership is essential.

Bad leadership can be detrimental to an organization. I hope you never have to experience working for or working with a bad leader. If you do, hopefully you will pick up some good advice in this book that may help you navigate through that situation.

> *"You learn far more from negative leadership than from positive leadership. Because you learn how not to do it. And, therefore, you learn how to do it."*
>
> **General Norman Schwarzkopf**

Bad Leadership - Work Page

1 Have you ever worked for a bad leader?

   Yes: ____   No: ____

2 What made this individual "bad"?

3 Did you stay and work with this bad leader or did you leave?

4 How can you ensure you won't end up being a bad leader?

6
LEADING BY EXAMPLE

Effective leaders lead by example. You must be willing to do what you are asking your team members to do. If you wouldn't do it, don't expect them to do it. Your team should be able to look at you and determine how to act and behave in situations. Leading by example means that you are going to work and live by the standards you establish for your team members. If you expect your team or organization to be at work by 7:30 each morning, then you be at work by 7:30 each morning. If you make them adhere to a certain dress code, then you need to adhere to the same code.

Don't tell them, show them. They are watching.

Leading by example is a leadership style. It means you are guiding your team(s) by modeling the behavior and work ethic that you expect them to have. In return, it inspires them to do the same as you. If you are putting the company's best interests first, then you could expect your team members to do the same without even having to tell them.

Leading by example will result in gaining further respect from your team and a better cohesiveness within your group. Be willing to get your hands dirty and work beside your team. This is extremely important for "front line" supervisors and leaders and will make them feel that you actually understand and appreciate the work that they are doing. By doing this, you will also be able to understand any barriers or issues they are facing that you can help them overcome.

Lead with that "follow me" attitude. Be that person your team can depend on to get them to that next level, or get them out of a slump. Be that person that they look to for inspiration and motivation.

Leading by example is a common trait that most successful leaders I have studied and interviewed have. It tends to be high up on their priority scale when describing how to be an effective leader. If you aren't doing this, start immediately. Be the kind of leader that you would follow.

> "What you do has far greater impact than what you say."
>
> **Stephen Covey**

Leading By Example - Work Page

1 Do you currently lead your team by example?

   Yes: _____   No: _____

2 Do leaders that you admire lead by example?

   Yes: _____   No: _____

3 Do you think leading by example is a quality that a good leader should have?

   Yes: _____   No: _____

4 Do you ask your team members to do work that you wouldn't do?

   Yes: _____   No: _____

7

SURROUND YOURSELF WITH LIKEMINDED PEOPLE - SO IMPORTANT!

While you are focused on reaching your next level of success, you must stay away from people who will distract you, bring you down, and derail your progress. It never ceases to amaze me the number of people who will try to place doubt in your head and give you negative vibes only because they are unsure how to do exactly what you are doing. These people are unhappy and want everyone else to be as unhappy as them. Distance yourself from people who lie to you, disrespect you, use you or put you down. Stay away!

Surround yourself with others who are on the same path to success. You want to be sure that the people closest to you support your dreams and will only encourage you to reach your goals. Surround yourself with people who inspire, motivate, and challenge you. This doesn't just mean the people at work or on your team, this means family and friends also. Keep negativity and toxic people away. Sometimes we must make hard decisions to cut people out of our lives. That isn't easy to do. But it is necessary if you are serious about your progress and committed to your success.

I recently had to remove someone from my inner circle that was toxic to my wellbeing. It was not easy for me. This person at one time was a good friend of mine. I started to find out everything about him was a lie. It was bad. He was a complete fraud, and I didn't know if he was the person he was presenting himself to be. I thought about it a long time, for months actually. I made up my mind that I needed to not only do this for my sanity, but I needed to distance myself from him for my reputation and my company's reputation. So, that is what I did. It was hard in the beginning, but once I did it and moved on, it gave me so much peace. I was able to focus more clearly without the negativity and distractions. I call this, "taking out the garbage".

When I say to take out the garbage, I am referring to removing any negative thoughts that are getting in your way of succeeding. Remove negativity, remove naysayers, remove doubt, remove fear, remove regret, and remove worry. These things can be absolutely detrimental to your progression. Eliminate all distractions. Any thought that clouds your mind or makes you second guess your worth is just getting in the way. You must learn to trust your abilities and take the necessary actions to increase your chances of being great. Do not let worry or fear get in your way. Sometimes putting yourself out there can make you feel vulnerable and open to criticism. During these times you must be courageous and keep moving forward. Being anxious or nervous is common. You've never put forth this amount of energy to guarantee your success before. So, there are going to be some uneasy feelings. But, due to your commitment to yourself, there is no turning back. You've already made the commitment to your success, so recommitting when things get tough and pushing through those obstacles will make it feel even better when you reach the top.

This garbage can take on many different forms, but one of the worst roadblocks in your path to success can be naysayers if you let them. These people are a drag and can bring you down to their level if you aren't careful. There are people in this world that don't want to put forth the effort to be successful, so they make fun of those people who ARE putting forth the effort. They try to make you doubt yourself and your goals. You have to cut these people out of your life. This is so important. It can be hard, especially if they are family or friends, but you have to limit your interaction with those people. You are on a different path now and have no time to listen to negativity. For some reason, they feel it's important for you to be just as unsuccessful as them. Remove them from your equation and keep moving forward.

By clearing this clutter and garbage you now have space to fill with positivity and more room to allow yourself to grow.

I'm sure you've heard the saying; you are the average of the five people you are around the most. Take a look around you. I asked you in your prework to write these five people down.

Look at that list. Who do you surround yourself with? Do your top five push you forward or pull you back? If your top five are doing you more harm than good, it's time to reevaluate your circle. I like to keep my circle filled with people who challenge me to do better. I need to be pushed and held accountable. I try to be that same person for them as well. You are meant for greater things, and you are on your way to achieving them. Stay positive, stay focused, and keep marching forward!

> "Stay away from negative people, they have a problem for every solution."
>
> **Albert Einstein**

Likeminded People - Work Page

List 5 people that are a positive influence in your life that contribute to your success:

1.
2.
3.
4.
5.

Reach out and thank each one of these people. Put a check mark next to their names above after you have spoken with them and truly thanked them.

Would you be on this list if someone else in your network was filling in the blanks? Be sure you are! You want to spread positivity and praise to others in your network. Be that person that they want to share good news with and that person they call for advice. This will come back to you 10-fold.

8

"LET THEM"

I recently attended a church with my family where Jordan Applebe, a close friend, is the minister. The sermon he covered during the program really hit home. It made me think of this book and how perfectly his words fit into this section. The sermon was titled "Let Them". And it was simple, but impactful. "Let Them" means just that; let them.

When naysayers, $hit talkers, and gossipers talk about you, make fun of you, call you names, and try to derail you, your reaction should be simple; let them. Instead of wasting your energy on negativity and trying to please everyone, just let those people say whatever they feel they need to say. Let them waste their time and energy trying to make you look bad instead of concentrating on their success. Let them look at you with jealousy and envy and attempt to knock you down. Just let them. The people that should matter to you won't judge you. The people you should care about should be lifting you up and supporting you. Let those other people talk. Just let them.

Just let them.

9

COMPARING YOURSELF TO OTHERS

This section is a big one for me. I had the hardest time with this for years. I would compare myself to friends, family, or even people I just met and get frustrated if I felt I wasn't at that level professionally. But what I wasn't considering was that everyone is on their own individual path. Those people were going through their own struggles and dealing with their own frustrations.

When I would compare myself to other people, it would always make me feel like a failure or I wasn't progressing fast enough. It would place doubt in my head and made me second guess what I was attempting to do. It affected my confidence and made me somewhat bitter at my situation.

It wasn't until years later when I looked back on that period in my life, that I realized how blind I was. In some ways those people were probably looking at me and thinking that I was at a level of success where they wanted to be. But regardless, it wasted time and energy that I could have used to better my situation.

Comparison is a thief of joy. This quote famously said by Theodore Roosevelt couldn't be more accurate. It will drag you down if you let it. Life is a marathon, not a sprint. Work hard and be the best version of you that you can possibly be.

> "Comparison is the thief of joy."
> **Theodore Roosevelt**

Comparing yourself to others hinders growth, especially when you are comparing yourself to others via social media. What others put on social media is the absolute best version of them; often, it is exaggerated or an outright lie. I'm sure your social media feeds are a lot like mine. Don't waste your time being envious of others by looking at their posts. Stop scrolling. The majority of those posts are not those people's real life. It is easy to fake happiness and success online.

The only person you are truly in competition with is the person you were yesterday. If you are better than you were yesterday, then you are winning. If you are progressing each day toward your goals, then you are winning. If you are getting closer to your dreams, then you are winning. Don't look at others and wish you had what they have. You are an original. Be you. Be your best version. Be better than you were yesterday. Steady progress equals success.

Comparing Yourself To Others - Work Page

1 Do you compare yourself to other people?

Yes: ____   No: ____

2 Who do you compare yourself to and why?

3 Does comparing yourself to other people help you reach your goals?

Yes: ____   No: ____

10

PATIENCE IS A VIRTUE

Patience - a simple Google of the word brings you to this definition: *the capacity to accept or tolerate delay, trouble, or suffering without getting angry or upset.* Without patience you can lose focus. It delays progress. It's easy to get frustrated and angry. Just because someone else may seem like they are moving more rapidly than you doesn't mean you aren't making progress. A lot of times, we feel like we should be further along than we are at this very moment. But you are in this very moment for a reason. You are right where you belong. Be persistent with your goals, but remain patient.

Have you ever heard of the phrase; *patience is a virtue?* Have you ever wondered what it meant exactly? The definition is being able to wait for something—to wait for a difficult time to pass or to wait for what you really want to happen instead of *going for instant gratification and settling for less sooner—is an admirable quality.*

Patience is something that is learned over time, at least it was for me. I'm not sure anyone is born with a patience gene. I wasn't. But patience is very important in the overall equation to a successful life. Success takes time to cultivate. Hard work, consistency, hustling, grinding, networking, collaborating are all part of the path to success. But it doesn't happen overnight. Doing those things on a regular basis over time will get you where you want to be. Don't try to rush it. Put in the work. But be patient. Your time will come.

11
THE POWER OF CONFIDENCE

There is one thing that people absolutely cannot fake no matter who you are. Confidence. You can easily tell if someone is confident with themselves and their abilities. Confidence is a feeling of self-assurance and appreciation for your abilities and qualities. Good leaders are confident in their decision-making skills, their processes, and their knowledge. Confidence is one of the most important parts of being a good leader. Confidence is powerful. You can gain a lot of respect with that one trait. Knowing your industry, product, and/or service is extremely important. But more importantly, having confidence in your own personal abilities is crucial.

Have you ever seen a public speaker who is so nervous that they appear unprepared and unassured of themselves? I've been at a national convention where an individual was paid $50K to speak to the group as the keynote speaker for 1 hour. He had just written a New York Times Bestseller book and was considered a subject matter expert in his field. But as he took the stage, it was apparent that this was going to be the longest 1 hour of his life. I'm not sure if it was due to insufficient rehearsal time, or if he was just a better writer than he was a public speaker, but the time he spent on stage was excruciating. Everything he said was lacking confidence and conviction. It was almost like he was seeking the audience's approval. It was so bad in fact that the organization requested half of the $50K back. Obviously, he knew the topic he was presenting. He was a well-established, well-known subject matter expert in his field. But because he was lacking confidence on stage, he came across as unprepared, unrehearsed, unassured, and honestly if you didn't know any better you would have thought he was brand new to the industry.

This is an extreme example of someone lacking confidence, but some people in the same situation are leading groups in organizations right now. And what's worse than lacking confidence as a leader, are the people who this individual is leading. What do you think happens when a leader isn't confident with themselves or their decisions? The group they are leading will lack confidence as well.

You want to ooze confidence out of your pores. People should believe you when you open your mouth. Confidence doesn't mean that you know every answer to every question. What it means is that you are confident enough to get through those tough questions or obstacles without looking like a deer in headlights. Be unapologetically, you. Be confident in yourself, your experiences, your knowledge, your education, your wisdom, and your abilities. Be comfortable being yourself. That is confidence. You will gain more respect by being authentic than by pretending to be something you aren't. Be confident in you.

Be Unapologetically, you!

Confidence is powerful. It's what attracts us to the greats. It's what draws us in and keeps us captivated by leaders. Some people describe confidence as mental fitness. The more you know your subject, the more you practice your public speaking, the more you study, the more you discuss, the more you read, the more you listen, the more you observe, the more confidence you will have. By being confident in yourself and your leadership abilities, your team will work with more confidence. They will feed off your passion and enthusiasm. They will believe in you and your decision-making skills. They will follow you with pride. Everyone appreciates and respects a confident leader.

> *"All you need in this life is ignorance and confidence, and then success is sure."*
>
> **Mark Twain**

12
LEADERS ARE DECISIVE

Being confident will help you make decisions. Good leaders are typically fast decision makers. Their experience, knowledge, and confidence lead them to make decisions faster than those who are less sure of themselves. Being indecisive can hold up an organization and cost the company money and time.

Early in my career, it took me a lot longer to make important decisions. I was afraid to mess up. I was afraid to fail or make the wrong decision. But as time went on, decisions became easier for me to make.

Not all decisions are the right decisions. But I make decisions based on facts and past experiences and leave emotions and ego out. One of the things people admire most about good leaders is their decision-making skills. I've sat down with several individuals who worked at various organizations and asked them very direct questions about their current leaders and managers. Most, if not all, were impressed by the decision-making skills of their "good" leaders. When leaders doubt their own abilities to make decisions, it creates doubt in the people around them. This leads to others not being confident in your abilities.

When making a decision, especially a decision that will affect the company and individuals who work there, you should be sure you are looking at the potential solutions with several factors in mind. You first need to listen carefully and ensure you understand the facts. Listening and understanding is part of being a good leader. Have an open mind without your ego or pride swaying you one way or another. Understand the consequences of whatever choice you make. How will this impact the company or the employees? Does this decision align with the company's vision, mission, and culture? If you are in a position to make important decisions for the company or a group of people, then obviously you have past experiences to rely on.

Use those experiences when making your decisions. Use experiences of other people that you have observed. How did those decisions affect those situations? Some decisions may require some collaboration between your team(s) or leadership group. Using team collaboration could spark different conversations leading to a decision you may not have thought of on your own. But one of the most important things to keep in mind when making an important decision is time management. Good leaders can get to a decision quickly. No matter how important that decision is, a leader will find a way to make a decision without wasting time and resources. In most cases, an important decision needs to be made fairly quickly. This is something you must master. You have to be confident in any decision you make, even if others do not agree with the decision. After you make the decision, lead the effort with confidence. By you being confident in your decision, it will demonstrate to others that they should be confident in that decision as well.

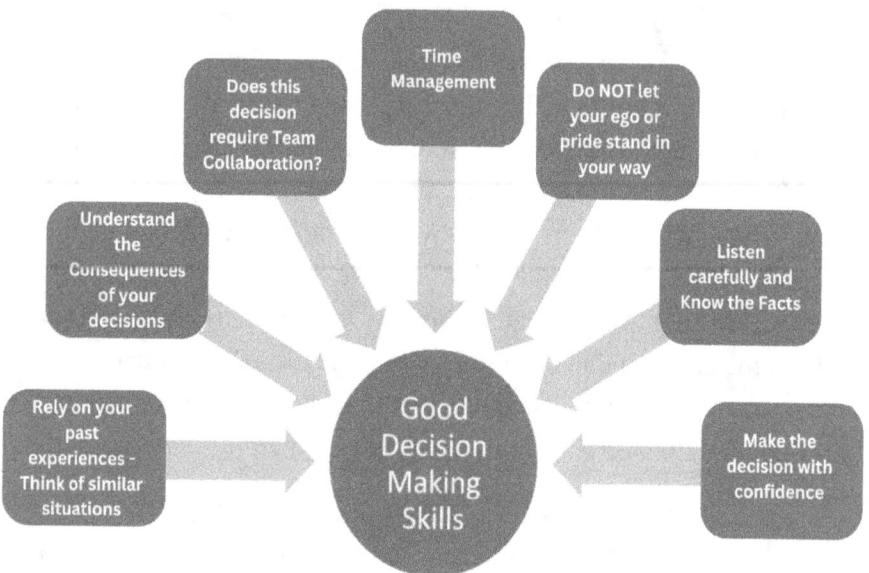

"You cannot make progress without making decisions."

Jim Rohn

13

PUBLIC SPEAKING

Public speaking can be scary for some people. The thought of being in front of dozens, hundreds, or even thousands of people can be intimidating. I know many people who are good at many things, but can't public speak. They are deathly afraid to get in front of people. They feel vulnerable and are too worried about messing up. That's a shame because there are a lot of people who could benefit from hearing about their experiences.

It was very hard for me when I first started getting in front of crowds and speaking. I rehearsed every line 100 times before getting on stage and rarely strayed from my script. I remember being on stage and not remembering what I just said because I was so nervous. My throat would close up and I could barely swallow. It would take me at least 5 minutes or more before I would finally calm down and be able to loosen up.

One consistent thing about me is that I always like tackling my fears head on. I would purposely volunteer for public speaking engagements to put myself in those situations so I could get better. I knew the only way I could overcome that fear was to face it. I would speak in meetings, at events, in front of high school and college students and anything else I could get into. Each time I did it I felt myself getting more comfortable and excited to get on stage rather than trying to hide when it was my turn to go up. The better I got at it, the more fun it became.

The closest thing I can compare it to is playing sports. The spotlight is on you and it's time to show them what you got! I absolutely love it now.

I knew that public speaking was going to be a big part of my career, and if I wanted to succeed, I would need to conquer my fear of stage fright. I know I'm not alone and most people have this same fear. There is not much better advice I can give about this topic besides how important it is to face it and hopefully eventually overcome it. You have to practice. Nothing else will get you over stage fright better than actually doing it as much as you possibly can. Start with small groups in meetings—volunteer for presentations or to lead a committee. As you get more comfortable with being in front of groups, you can start volunteering for bigger venues.

Speaking in front of a group or organization is essential if you plan on being a successful leader. It would be shameful if you avoided this fear your entire career when it will hold you back from progressing. This will be hard at first, but it will get easier each time you do it. And soon, you will start enjoying it. Public speaking can be fun. Especially if it's over a topic you are familiar with and passionate about. The goal is to practice and get in front of people as much as possible. Write it down in your planner and start making an intentional effort to practice.

> *"All the great speakers were bad speakers first."*
>
> **Ralph Waldo Emerson**

Public Speaking - Work Page

1 Do you have stage fright?

   Yes: _____   No: _____

2 What is your greatest fear about public speaking?

3 What is the largest group you have spoken to?

4 What was the topic that you covered during that presentation?

5 Does your current job or business require you to speak in front of groups of people?

   Yes: _____   No: _____

6 Are there any public speakers that you admire or look up to? If so, who?

Yes: _____   No: _____

7 In your opinion, what is the most important trait a public speaker should have?

14

SETTING GOALS - WAKING UP WITH A PURPOSE

Do you have goals that you are working towards? Do you have long-term goals or short-term goals, or both?

Do you set goals for your team?

I'm hoping you answered yes to all the above. Goals are necessary. Without goals, you are kind of just blowing in the wind. You need things that keep you in line and focused on the bigger picture. You need benchmarks or ways to measure whether you and your team are making progress. These goals become your timeline and a way of holding yourself and your team accountable. Write your goals down, and plan for improvement each day. Plans are your predictions for the future. Each morning you should wake up with a purpose. What's on my agenda today? What goals am I striving for today? How will

I achieve my goals today? Daily goals are a great method to use to keep a steady pace and inch closer and closer to your bigger long-term goals. Setting daily goals for you and your team gives you a measurable range of success and holds you accountable each day for progressing towards something larger. Don't be afraid to celebrate meeting those short daily goals, those are achievements. It's good to stay positive, stay motivated, and count each time you hit a new level of success.

> *"A goal without a timeline is just a dream."*
>
> **Robert Herjavec**

I use a daily planner for every day of my life. I set long-term, high-level goals that push me and bring out the best in me. There aren't any unrealistic goals, but there are unrealistic timelines. Each day you want to set high-level, short-term goals, but you also need to keep in mind the bigger target you are trying to hit. Writing down your BIG GOALS and being forced to look at them and review them each day will keep you on track and hold you accountable in your daily progress. If you don't have a daily planner, I suggest getting one and starting to use it immediately. Or, if you are more of a techy person than I am, download a planner app on your phone. I like using the old-fashioned pen and paper, but whatever works for you is fine. But start using a planner. It's a true accountability log that should be used each day of the week, even weekends.

I review my planner each evening and write down my

achievements. What did I accomplish today? What did my team accomplish today? And then, I plan the next day's events. Networking and self-improvement are part of each one of my days. It's important for me to gain new relevant contacts but also to remain close to my already established contact list. If you haven't talked to someone who you feel is important in a while, plan time to pick up the phone and give them a call. Keep those individuals close to you. We all need contacts that we can rely on for certain things from time to time.

Self-improvement is part of my daily life, and I set aside time for it each day. Whether it is a book, an online seminar, a webinar, a conference, listening to a podcast, an online course or attending a lecture ... I always make time to continue to learn. A leader should never stop learning. It's something that will set you apart from the competition. Plan for it.

When setting goals for your team each week, be sure you not only meet with them at the beginning of the week to go over those goals but also meet with them at the end of the week to discuss their achievements. Weekly goal setting is a great tool to keep your team motivated and on track. The weekly goals need to be realistic but high enough that they must work hard to hit those levels. It's even good to get them involved and develop a couple of group goals themselves. This will make them feel more needed, appreciated, and part of the team.

Celebrate small victories. Be proud of yourself and your team for reaching those milestones. The goal is to keep moving forward. Be strategic with the goals you set for yourself. Make sure when you are planning your day that those plans are relevant towards your bigger end game. Each goal should be intentional and with a clear direction in mind.

Here's an example of one of my inserts from my daily planner. This is a real day out of my planner within the past year, although I did take out all names of individuals and companies. This example does not include my short-term or long-term goals. Those are typically at the top of my planner and not listed in the daily "task" sections.

6.30 am:	Walk 3 miles; listen to podcast
8 am:	Phone call with colleague to discuss next month's committee meeting
8.30 am:	Follow-up interview with potential employee
9.30 am:	Virtual meeting with publisher to discuss next steps
10 am:	Work on training program for company A
11 am:	Weekly phone call with mentor
12 pm:	Lunch with potential customer
1.30 pm:	Catch up on emails and phone calls
3 pm:	Meeting with Leadership Team
4.30 pm:	Work on proposal for Company B
6 pm:	Company networking event
8 pm:	Prepare for tomorrow
9.30 pm:	In bed by 9:30 pm

As you can tell, my planner isn't anything special. But it keeps me on track, and each time I cross one of my daily tasks off it gives me a sense of accomplishment. I do the same thing for weekends as well. I don't let weekends pass me by without doing something that gets me closer to my goals. Just because those two days don't fall on a "normal" 5-day work-week, doesn't mean you are supposed to take them off. I do allow myself more freedom on the weekends and use the weekends to do most of my writing and learning. But regardless, I plan each day of my life using a planner. It's been hugely beneficial for me, and I'm not sure I could go about my day without doing it at this point.

Get yourself a planner. Make sure your team members are using a planner. Start filling in the blanks and crossing off achievements. Wake up with a purpose every day. This will keep you on track, help you stay focused, and ultimately improve your daily productivity to ensure you are making the progress you need to reach your goals.

Setting Goals - Work Page

1 Do you currently use a daily planner or app that helps you stay on track throughout the day?

Yes: _____   No: _____

2 Do you celebrate small victories?

Yes: _____   No: _____

3 What are your 3 personal BIG life goals?

1.
2.
3.

4 Where do you see yourself in 10 years?

5 How will you get there?

6 What are your 3 BIG goals for your team?

1.
2.
3.

7 What are your 3 short-term goals for your team?

1.
2.
3.

8 How will you ensure your team stays on track to reach their goals?

15

MAKE GOOD CHOICES - MGC

Each day, when my son walks out of the house for school, work, or to hang out with his friends, the last thing I say to him is "Make Good Choices". I've taught my kids from an early age that each choice you make in life has a consequence. Good choices usually mean there are good consequences. Bad choices usually mean bad consequences. It's not rocket science, but it's a fact. The more good choices you make, the more good things start happening to you and vice versa. You are the sum of your choices.

Each day, we are all faced with decisions we need to make. We come to a fork in the road that requires us to turn left or right. Think about your "why" before each decision is made. Does this benefit your "why"? Does this help you progress towards your goals? Is this a healthy decision, or am I just being lazy? If we stay true to ourselves and do the right thing, good things will come back to us most of the time. When you look at people who are successful, or people who haven't achieved much success at all, most of the time those people end up in those situations due to life choices they each made for themselves. Your life is typically a direct result of the choices you have made. If you don't like where your life is right now, it is time to start making better choices to secure a better future. We must make good choices all the time.

If we consistently make good choices and choose the right path to travel, then there is no doubt that we will end up right where we belong. Start choosing actions that are in your best interest. Successful people have made many good choices, day in and day out. Do your own research with successful people that you know. And then research those who aren't successful. You will typically discover that each of those people is a result of the decisions they have made along the way. Make good choices and stay consistent. This is important for you as an individual and as a leader of a team, an organization, or even your family. Get into the habit of asking yourself if this decision supports your path to success.

> Does this decision support my path to success?

16

HOLDING YOURSELF ACCOUNTABLE
- COMMIT TO YOUR OWN SUCCESS

As I stated in the "MGC" section, you are the result of your past behaviors and choices. Holding yourself accountable is the only way you will be able to ensure you make good decisions moving forward. Don't blame others for you not being at the level you want to be. Look in the mirror and blame that person. Being able to blame yourself instead of others is a sign of maturity. You are the only person that determines your outcome. Let that sink in.

If you haven't studied the *Locus of Control* concept, I highly recommend you do so. This concept was developed by Julian B Rotter in 1954. It states that there are three different kinds of people; those who have a strong internal locus of control believe they are the result of their own actions, and those with a strong external locus of control blame external factors for their situations. There is also a third locus of control called a Bi-local. These individuals contain a mix of both external and internal types. The study dives into a lot more details, but I challenge you to do your own research and figure out what lane you fall in. If you tend to lean more towards the external locus of control, I would make a conscious effort to start taking some accountability in your life.

Blaming others for your current situation or for your failures is just an excuse. Undoubtedly, you have already overcome obstacles in your life to be where you are today. There is no doubt that you will have to overcome a lot more obstacles in the future. We all do. Blaming others or blaming other external factors for not being as successful as you want to be will only hold you back further. When you reach an obstacle, your first thought process should be on how to get through it. Not throw a pity party. Because I promise you, nobody gives a shit.

It's always good to do some self-reflection. You need to understand what got you to where you are today and what you can do differently to change the outcome of your next 5 – 10 years. Evaluate yourself. This should be a daily process. At the end of the day, you are the only one you can truly count on to get you to where you want to be. You can do anything you want if you give it the right amount of effort. Nobody else can or will do this for you.

17

CONTINUE LEARNING

Planning continuous education in your life will set you apart from the majority of the pack. A lot of people do not attempt to grow themselves mentally. So, they become stagnant. Continue to learn. Keep a hunger for growth. Educating yourself does not necessarily mean getting a college degree. It means read a book, take a course, attend a seminar, listen to an educational podcast, or anything that pushes you to use your brain. Human beings are sponges. We should be learning something new every day. Don't underestimate the power of education. Continue to invest in your personal development; it is the bridge that takes you from where you are – to where you want to be. This is the best investment you can make for yourself.

One of my favorite things to do is listen to podcasts while I drive or take walks in the morning. It makes me think and sparks new ideas and creativity. Even if I don't necessarily agree with the person speaking, that's ok. Listening to other people's opinions will push you to open up your mind to other possibilities. We are all humans, but each one of us is very different. If you are not growing, you are falling behind.

My go-to motivational guy has to be ET! I love Eric Thomas. The passion that he brings to his speaking engagements and podcasts is unbelievable. I listen to him at least 3 or 4 times per week, usually when working out or driving. Every time I listen to him, he sparks a new idea for me. For leadership podcasts, I usually listen to Jordan Peterson or Simon Sinek. I've also listened to and watched almost every Ted Talk on YouTube. And of course, Gary V and Patrick Bet-David are always on my playlist. I learn something new from these guys constantly. Listening to successful people talk about their successes and failures makes you realize they are human, just like us. Each one of us has the ability to be great. Continuing your education is just one of the ways that can help you get there. Attend a seminar about a topic that you usually wouldn't care about.

Learn a new language. Learn how to play an instrument. Do research on world leaders you admire. Read biographies of successful people to determine how they got to where they are. Go to company meetings that aren't in your specific area of expertise. Visit other departments and learn some of their processes. Just learn. Remember, confidence is considered mental fitness. Use your brain. Expand your horizons. Travel - learn other cultures by visiting them - this is an education that can't be taught in a classroom. But whatever you do, don't stop learning and yearning for knowledge. As your knowledge, experience, and skills grow, so will your worth in the marketplace. You, all of a sudden, are now on a different playing field. This leads to new job opportunities, business ventures, and partnerships. Continuing your education will speed up your progress. Put in the time and effort to be better.

18

BARRIERS: RELENTLESS PROGRESSION

I'm sure you have overcome several barriers and obstacles to get where you are today. We all have. I'm sure it hasn't been easy, nothing worth it ever is. But do you know what the barriers and obstacles are that are keeping you from reaching your next desired level of success? Have you determined what is stopping you? I can answer that for you if you don't know. It's you! Once you realize that your dream of being a Doctor, Lawyer, business owner, department manager, real estate developer or whatever you aspire to be, is absolutely achievable, nothing should stand in your way.

I could never stand it when one of my kids would say, "I will try". That, to me, is an immediate copout. Saying, "I will try", means you are leaving room for failure. I will try, really means that I might fail. Make your mind up that you WILL accomplish whatever you want, and start working towards that goal, and never quit.

> ~~I WILL TRY~~ - NO, I WILL

Relentless Progression is something I have been preaching for years. In its simplest of terms, it means that you progress each day without making any excuses. Each day, you get one step closer to your ultimate goals, whatever they may be. Progression is success. Relentless is not letting anything stand in your way. Once you determine the desired outcome, focus on that at each moment of your day, and make it happen. There should be no excuses, nothing standing in your way, and no reason you can't reach your goals.

This may come off a little rude, but if you haven't already, you will learn that winners win, and losers lose. This doesn't mean getting first place in everything you do. Winning and losing is a mentality. It's a way of life. Those who don't make excuses and continue to progress even in the face of adversity and unbelievable obstacles, are winners. Those who continue to make excuses and continue to whine and complain about their situation without making any effort to overcome it, are losers. The losers will never be winners. They will keep complaining and drag you right down with them if you let them. The winners are going to win. It's simple. They will keep moving forward, overcome obstacles, keep learning, keep working hard, and make good choices, and they will win.

Work on having a "winner" mentality.

It's how I live my life. I set my goals each day, and I work my ass off until I reach those goals. I work better with small goals that will result in a bigger outcome. But I enjoy celebrating small daily victories. You should be almost obsessive about reaching your goals. Work so hard that people think you are crazy. Big effort means big progress. Big progress means big results. Be addicted to your own progress.

Don't set limitations for yourself. Trust yourself, your intuition, abilities, experience, and determination to succeed.

You will face barriers and roadblocks throughout your days that will try to deter you from reaching your wanted level of success. But instead of giving up or making excuses, march forward and run right through those obstacles. They are merely just that ... obstacles. They aren't dead ends. Nothing worth it will be easy. Make up your mind right now that you won't make excuses for not reaching your goals. Tell yourself right now that nothing will get in your way. Each decision you make, each obstacle you overcome, each moment of your life, you are getting closer to your big goals.

Set your goals BIG. Don't settle!

The only thing that can stop you - is you. Think about that statement. Then think about what you consider barriers in your path to success. I bet if you are completely honest with yourself, you can figure out a way to get around everything that is "stopping" you from getting to that next level. Listen,

I know some people have the cards stacked against them, and I completely understand that some people will have to work harder to achieve their goals than others. But ... ok. Do it. Don't be a victim, and don't be a complainer. Just get your mind right, focus on your big goals, and start marching forward. Life isn't fair and it's never going to be fair, so come to terms with that and get moving!

This is the most important thing you can do as a leader and as someone trying to reach the next level of success. You will never reach your full potential if you continue to get sidetracked, disengaged, and off-course. Steady progress **is** success. Without it, you are fighting a losing battle. Any so-called barrier or obstacle that is beyond your control, you shouldn't worry about. If you can't control it, you can't change it, so you will have to overcome it. Keep marching forward!

> *"If you can't fly then run, if you can't run then walk, if you can't walk then crawl, but whatever you do you have to keep moving forward."*
>
> **Martin Luther King Jr**

In the past couple of decades, we have seen the economy go from great to bad, then bad to worse. We've had pandemics, we've had racial division, we've had unstable political conditions, and we've had economic uncertainty. But, conditions like these are what separates the average from the beasts!

During these times of duress and uncertainty, people have created opportunities for themselves. We have seen new companies popup, organizations pivot their services or products, and people lose their jobs during the chaos and open successful businesses.

Being a leader means knowing how to pivot and not make excuses. If you come across what most would consider an unbeatable obstacle, run right through that mother$%#!@!!!! Consider it a challenge and destroy it! *(Figuratively speaking of course)*

You will have to go through it to get to it.

The only thing that will ever get in my way of achieving my goals is me. I don't care who the president is, I don't care what others think about my dreams and goals, I don't care what is happening in China, there will be nothing that will stop me from accomplishing what I want to accomplish.

This is RELENTLESS PROGRESSION!

Remember the two basic rules to a successful life:

Rule #1: Never Quit!
Rule #2: Always Remember Rule #1!

Blaze your own path and watch others follow. Be a leader, make good choices, and keep marching forward. Relentless progression is my definition of success! Being closer to your BIG DREAM than you were yesterday is something to be proud of. If you achieve that on a daily basis, imagine how close you would be one year from now, five years from now, 8 years from now! Relentless Progression! No excuses! Nothing replaces determination and hard work!

> *"The secret to handling changes is to focus on progress. If you can make progress on a regular basis, then you feel alive."*
>
> **Tony Robbins**

Barriers - Work Page

1 What are you going to allow to stop you from reaching your goals?

2 List 3 obstacles in your life right now that you need to overcome.

1.
2.
3.

3 How will you overcome those obstacles?

1.
2.
3.

4 Who is going to determine your success?

_____

5 Who is responsible for your success?

_____

6 Will excuses help you achieve success?

Yes: _____   No: _____

7 Does complaining help you achieve success?

   Yes: _____   No: _____

8 Is it a good idea to give up if things get hard or don't go your way?

   Yes: _____   No: _____

9 How do you know when it is a good time to quit?

   _____

10 Will you let other people stand in your way of your own success?

   Yes: _____   No: _____

19

BE A COMPLETER

The title of this section says it all. And it goes hand in hand with *Relentless Progression* that you read earlier in the book. *Be a Completer.* It's simple. If you start something, finish it. Leaders finish things. They don't walk away halfway through something. They don't abandon ship when things get hard. A leader will initiate a process, own the process, complete the process, and most importantly, own the results, whether good or bad. Good leaders don't pass the blame on to other people, especially those you lead.

If the results aren't what you expected or wanted, you still need to take responsibility for that outcome. You oversaw and were responsible for the process, so take ownership of the results. Leaders complete. This doesn't mean you have to do it on your own. Utilize your team members and experts but own and finish the process. You want the reputation of – *when you say something, you mean it.* When you say you are going to do something, you want everyone to believe you and know you won't stop until it is complete.

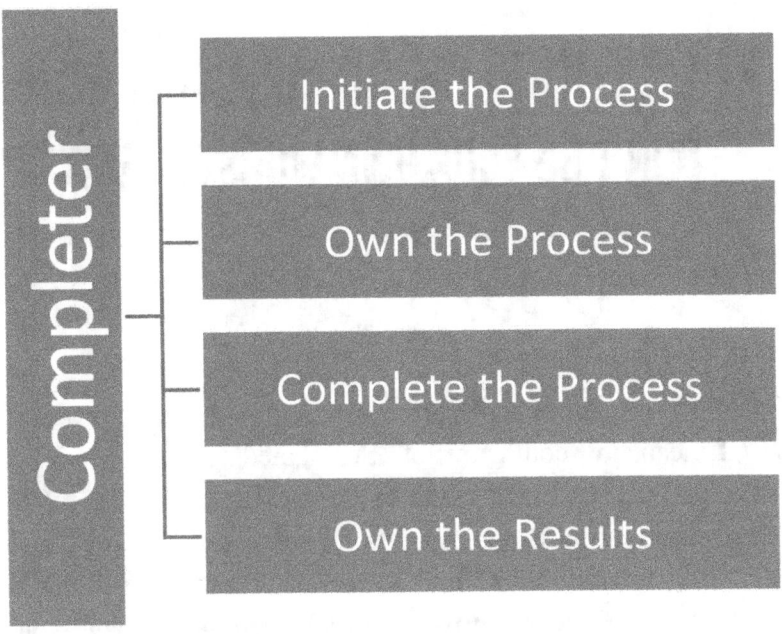

20

KEEP YOUR SOCIAL MEDIA CLEAN
- DON'T BE YOUR OWN WORST ENEMY

Most of us have some form of social media that we use. I mean, how could you not? Social media is how we market ourselves and our businesses. It's how we keep in touch with friends and family. But you can be your own worst enemy if you don't figure out how to control yourself or your posts. If you have posted things in the past that you feel may damage your reputation or any future endeavors, I would strongly suggest cleaning them up immediately. Your haters and nonbelievers love to screenshot those questionable posts and pictures, and once they do, it is forever out there in the world, no matter what you do.

Believe it or not, I can guarantee you have been Googled and researched online. Employers, coworkers, friends, family, or acquaintances have examined your social media posts. And people have judged you based on what they find online. Some people find it extremely hard not to post every single minute of their day online, whether it be good or bad. This can put an immediate halt to your career. Stay away from the "trolls", stay away from the hate fueled political posts, and stay away from being nasty or unprofessional.

It is very common for companies to do social media research on potential employees before interviewing or hiring them. I've seen this ruin people's chances of being hired several times. Don't let something silly set you back.

Making good choices should also relate to your social media activity, not just your "in-person" real life. If you have to think about it before you post it, it's probably not a good idea. Before doing anything online ask yourself, "Does this decision support my path to success?" If it doesn't, then don't do it.

21

WORK JUST A LITTLE BIT HARDER

With everything mentioned before this section, you need to understand the importance of hard work. My mom told my brother and I when we were growing up, that if you just work a little bit harder than everyone else, you will see the difference. It's true, good old-fashioned hard work should not be underestimated. Nothing can replace someone who is constantly moving and working and striving for better. It gives you the edge. Others will notice, and it will make them work harder, or it will weed out those people who are being left behind by laziness or complacency. You want to be the hardest-working individual in your position in your entire industry. You shouldn't lose business, a promotion, or a job opportunity because someone else is outworking you. That should be the last reason for you not to succeed. Put forth the extra effort. Go the extra mile. This will separate you from the pack.

Kobe Bryant is one of the best examples of this. He's famously known for his over-the-top work ethic. I listen to his videos and interviews from podcasts that he did after he retired from the NBA. He made it a mission that nobody else would outwork him. If he knew you were going to the gym to practice at 8 am, he would be there at 7. If you were going to stay late and work on your game, he would stay later.

His work ethic and determination to be the best he possibly could be, made him who we know today as one of the best basketball players to ever play the game. He sacrificed time and energy but will go down in history as one of the greatest.

His work ethic set an example for his teammates and made them work harder. He set the expectations. He also said that he studied the players who he looked up to and asked them how they became so successful. Michael Jordan was one of these players and famously became one of Kobe Bryant's mentors and friends. This falls in line with our observation and interviewing of successful leaders' sections.

> *"Great things come from hard work and perseverance. No excuses."*
>
> Kobe Bryant

As a leader, this is an excellent way to lead by example. When your team sees how hard you are working, it encourages them to put forth that extra effort as well. Be the example of what you expect from your team. Like my mom said, "work just a little bit harder".

22

CONSISTENCY

Now that we've discussed professionalism, continuing your education, leading by example, breaking down barriers, and making good choices, let's talk about consistency. Doing each of these things every now and then will not benefit you much, but doing them consistently will give you the results you are searching for. Remember, you ARE what you repeatedly do.

... you ARE what you repeatedly do!

Consistency is the key to success at anything and everything you do. Whether it's advancing your career, being a better partner to your spouse, raising your kids, trying to lose weight, or working towards your master's degree, to be successful you must maintain positive and consistent behavior.

> "Success isn't always about greatness. It's about consistency. Consistent hard work leads to success. Greatness will come."
>
> Dwayne Johnson

Athletes are a perfect example of good results from discipline and consistent positive behavior. Professional athletes, especially the greats, don't just show up on game day and dominate. They work every day to be the best they can be. They have a daily schedule with productive habits consisting of lifting weights, cardio workouts, studying opponents, eating healthy, and practicing their sport. They also set short-term team goals, consisting of winning this week's game, long-term goals, which consist of winning the championship or Superbowl, and a plethora of personal goals. An athlete is a team member, a leader, and their personal brand. If we all had the habits and focus that professional athletes have mastered, then we would all be successful at whatever venture we are involved in.

Since most of us are not professional athletes, we must think about the business we are in and the group of people we are leading. Becoming great at your craft takes time and a lot of effort. But you should make consistent and deliberate moves that help you and your team progress. Think about where you want to be in 5 years and how you will get there. What steps will you take to get closer to your goal each day? Each decision, each choice, and each move you make should be calculated and done with the intent of progressing. Small, consistent steps leading in the right direction will get you to your desired destination. Have patience. You don't become great overnight. You make deliberate, calculated, intentional, consistent actions that will win you small victories each day, which become significant victories over longer periods of time. It won't be overnight, but those small steps are inching you closer to making your dreams your reality.

> *"A journey of a thousand miles begins with a single step."*
>
> Lao-Tzu

The *Consistency Cycle* is an easy concept. It takes what you've learned already as well as some topics we have yet to cover, and simplifies it into an easy-to-use diagram. See below. When you look at these steps in a cycle like this, and it becomes part of your daily routine, there is no option but for you to progress as a leader and as a person. The cycle never stops. It goes 365 days a year. Consistency is key. You can replace some of the steps with your own steps or keep these steps and add additional steps. As long as you stay consistent, it will work. Build your own Consistency Cycle and use it. Put it in your daily planner or on your computer or iPad. You can even put it on your refrigerator door or bathroom mirror. It's a reminder of what you should do daily for progress. This, accompanied by your daily planner, should be your guide to each one of your days. There should be no doubt what you have to accomplish each day when you wake up if these two items are done correctly.

The Consistency Cycle is automatic. It will include the same information day in and day out. It's the big overall daily picture of what each one of your days looks like. The daily planner breaks down the individual days into smaller tasks. So, when you are building your Consistency Cycle, fill it in with those things you should be doing to improve your overall health, career, family, and goals. Don't get into the details, just fill it in with overarching generalized "to-do's" that will keep you on the straight and narrow. The goal is to hold yourself accountable towards your commitment to your success.

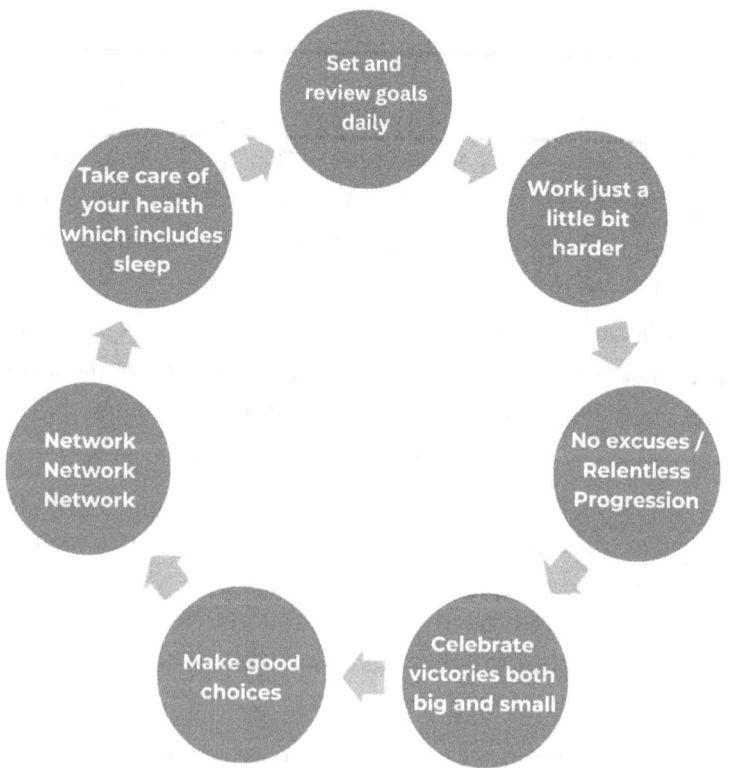

COMPLACENCY – NEVER BEING SATISFIED

There are a few things that truly successful and wealthy people have in common. And one of them that I've found common with every individual I've studied and interviewed is that none of them are ever satisfied. They are consistently moving forward and growing. Their minds all seem to be forward-thinking, all the time. It's hard to keep up. When you finally understand where they are headed, they are already off in a different direction. And, I don't mean scatterbrained, I mean they are laser focused but always moving.

Complacency can kill a business and can destroy your forward momentum. Always want more. Continue to improve yourself with education (seminars, college courses, webinars, reading books, etc), networking, and creating opportunities to grow. If you grow, then your team will grow. Expect the same forward progress from your team. Don't let them become complacent!

> *"Complacency is the last hurdle standing between any team and its potential greatness."*
>
> Pat Riley

No matter what level you are at in your career, you should always want more. Wanting more is not greed. Wanting more is not selfish. Successful people are mostly never satisfied. They believe in themselves and know they can reach the next level. Don't let anyone tell you wanting more for yourself and your family is greedy or selfish. Just because those people don't have the drive or determination that you have doesn't mean you are wrong. I always want more. I push myself every day of my life. I don't leave anything on the table.

A great example is what I'm doing at this very moment, writing a book. I've always enjoyed writing about my situations and life experiences. Over the years, I've gained quite a bit of knowledge on successful leadership, motivating teams, and inspiring others. I love to share what I've learned and what has worked well for me throughout my career. I've mentored dozens of people and always wanted to write some of it down on paper. So that's what I'm doing. It is truly rewarding when I help someone get to the next level of their career or simply find more happiness in their lives.

Wanting more is not bad. Push yourself to the limits—step outside of your "normal" box. I've left jobs because of the limitations set on me. You cannot hold me down and keep me from growing, period. I will get more. And you should feel the exact same way about yourself. Want more, get more, and don't let anyone get in your way.

23

THE ART OF SUCCESSFUL NETWORKING

Now let's talk about the importance of networking. Your talents and skills will only take you so far. At some point you will have to rely on your network of people to close that deal, to guarantee that promotion, to collaborate on a project, or to lean on when you are trying to get that new client. Networking is necessary. It is true what they say, it's not what you know, it's who you know.

As I mentioned previously, I was born with a knack for networking. It's easy for me to walk into a room and feel comfortable not knowing anyone. I'm a good bullshitter and can hang with the best. I've been able to turn a lot of these spontanous networking relationships into legit business relationships. But I understand not everyone is born with this ability, and it requires some extra effort. That's OK. There are several other areas of my life that I've had to work extra hard on to become successful, and networking just happens to be one of the things I'm good at.

Most people fear being rejected or feeling unworthy of being in a room where you don't know anyone. If this is something that challenges you, then I would suggest you start to practice as much as possible. There is no better way to overcome your lack of confidence or fear of rejection than practice every chance you get.

My dad used to say, "A man was walking around Boston looking for Fenway Park. He asked another man on the sidewalk, 'How do you get to Fenway?' The man answered, 'Practice, practice, practice'." This is true with everything in your life. Especially overcoming fears. The more times you are put into situations where you are uncomfortable, the better you will become at thriving in those situations.

Networking is an art. It's a process. It should be intentional and somewhat strategic. You meet someone, you exchange names, occupations, business cards, a little small talk, and then you move on. But what do you do with that information when you leave?

One of the things I do after every networking event I attend, I gather the business cards I collected, make notes on some, and categorize all of them into three different categories: high, mid, and low priority. The high and mid priorities I want to personally reach out to within the next couple of days, usually by email. I let them know it was a pleasure meeting them, and I look forward to working with them in the future. The low category contacts are usually people I know wouldn't be able to help me in my current endeavors, but I still want to keep in touch with.

So, I try to connect with all three categories on social media right away. For work, I use LinkedIn. To me, it's been the best networking platform for my business ventures that I've ever used. Once connected, you can start building a relationship by commenting, liking, and promoting those new contacts' posts and businesses.

A lot of times, being connected through social media opens new opportunities to collaborate on certain initiatives, which is also a great way to build relationships. Once you've contacted them by email or social media, don't lose contact. Keep in touch with them every now and then, especially your high and mid-level priority relationships.

This process may not be suitable for everyone, but it definitely works for me, and I've been doing it this way for years. But this will at least give you an idea of what it takes to make a networking event successful for you. You can always tweak your process, but be sure you HAVE a process. Be organized, be intentional, and practice.

"Your network is your net worth."

Porter Gale

I've also learned over the years to help others. Even if you think they won't be able to help you. I've done this so many times over the years, and it always turns out to be a positive experience for me. I will go out of my way to write reference letters for individuals looking for employment, or make a call to a business associate because I have a colleague trying to get a new contract, or volunteer to help on some of their initiatives that have nothing to do with my industry at all. This all comes back to me. People don't forget people who go out of their way to help them. Do this as often as you can. Look for opportunities to help others.

Another "must do" is to always be prepared to give your 30 second elevator speech. This needs to be well rehearsed and ready to be delivered to anyone at any time. Know exactly what you would say to someone if they were to question you about your company, your goals, or your ambitions. People respect individuals who are confident and sure of themselves. You don't want to look like a deer in headlights at a networking event when the person you are trying to build a relationship with questions you, and you can't provide an immediate answer. Be prepared. Practice this speech often to yourself and to others so you will nail it when the opportunity presents itself.

Put yourself out there. Network as often as you possibly can, especially early in your career. Set aside time for it and write it in your daily planner. Attend events and seminars, and get involved in extracurricular activities. Meet new people, establish new relationships, and make time to grow those relationships. I rely on other people daily to help me in my endeavors. It's necessary. I cannot imagine trying to do some of the things I do without knowing the right people.

Meeting new people and establishing new relationships is key but turning those relationships into business opportunities is the art you must master. The most well-connected people are usually the most successful people. Establish new relationships, build them up, and nurture them. Join committees, online platforms (be active), attend work-related events or extracurricular activities, get active in your alumni associations, volunteer at nonprofits, etc. The point is to get out there and let people know you exist. You need to remind them constantly that you are there. When an opportunity comes up in your field or area of expertise, they need to think of you immediately. Your name should be synonymous with your line of work.

Successful networking is not easy for some of us. But the worst mistake is to not network at all. The more you do it the more you will sharpen your skills and tactics, and the easier it will become.

As mentioned, It's easy to meet people, but developing your process of following up and taking that initial meeting to establish a working relationship is the art of networking. Develop your process, tweak it as you go, and practice as often as you can. The more you do it, the better you will become.

Network! Network! Network! Get moving!

24

SOFT SKILLS - THE BASICS

When you think of a leader you respect and admire, what are some of their characteristics and mannerisms? Are they sloppy dressers? Do they mumble when they speak? Are they consistently late? Are they rude or belittling? I would think that if you see this individual as a success story and have decided that they are what a leader should be, the answer to these questions would be no.

Finding good people with decent soft skills is harder to find these days. Let's make sure you aren't one of those statistics.

Unfortunately, there are times when individuals are put into certain leadership positions that should not be there. They either know someone in a higher position, or their superiors have turned a blind eye to that person's true characteristics. Either way, that is not the image you want to portray. You will never gain everyone's respect or approval, so don't strive for that. But you can carry yourself in a mature, professional, respectful manner, which should set an example to everyone else on how to act and behave.

COMMUNICATION

After working with and observing dozens of successful leaders throughout the years, it's obvious that all these individuals are good communicators. Several factors go into what makes a good, effective, well-rounded communicator. As a leader, you need to communicate effectively with people at all levels of an organization.

Communication is the exchanging of information and ideas. The first thing you need to understand before communicating, either in a team or one on one environment, is your audience. Your audience will determine how and what you communicate. It will also determine how you tailor your message, such as what technical language, jargon, slang or acronyms you can use.

It's essential to understand who you are communicating with, but also very important to understand who may end up being your secondary audience as well. Your secondary audience are people who may come across your message in an email, text, or social media post that weren't initially the target audience. You need to keep this group in mind anytime you are about to hit "send" or "post".

Speaking clearly and at a pace where the information is being absorbed by the receiver, where the individual you are communicating with completely understands the meaning behind your words or the direction you are giving them, is crucial. The last thing you want to do is have someone misinterpret your words and make a mistake that wastes time or resources or hurts someone. When talking with your team, a good suggestion and technique is to get them to repeat what you said or simply give you the meaning behind what you said to ensure everyone is on the same page. I use this technique several times a day when communicating to team members, employees, or even my kids. I want there to be no room for error or misinterpretation.

Being an effective listener is an important part of the communication process. When someone is speaking, be engaged, give feedback, look at them in their eyes, and let them know you are listening. Not all conversations will be as interesting as you would like, but actively participate in all of them as if they were. When I find myself in situations where I am bored or uninterested, I use that opportunity to practice my listening skills. It is part of being able to adapt to different situations.

One of the most critical elements of being a good communicator is having professional writing skills. The proper use of certain words, punctuation, and spelling is so important. I can't tell you how many times people have lost deals by sending me emails that look like a 3rd grader wrote it. I have zero tolerance for unprofessional emails that I must decipher to understand. If you do not have good writing skills, take a writing class at your local community college or a course online. Professional writing skills are important, especially in today's world, where most of our daily work communications are emails, texts, or through different applications such as Teams.

Before we move on to the next topic, I want to discuss an important communication element that needs recognition. When someone sends you an email, text or leaves you a voicemail … please respond! Even if it is a quick message that simply states that you received the email and will respond more thoroughly when you have time. Not acknowledging someone's attempt at reaching you is rude, disrespectful, and unprofessional. You may need a quick response from that individual later down the road, so it is good to keep a good communication dialogue between those who reach out. There is no excuse not to respond.

PUNCTUALITY

There are going to be times when you run late for meetings, it's going to happen. But do not get into the habit of being late. My grandfather always said, "Being 15 minutes early means you are on time, arriving on time means you are late.". It is a good habit to always plan on being early to anything that you are scheduled to attend. Prepare early, plan for the unexpected, and show up on time (15 minutes early). Being late means that you think your time is more valuable than the people you are meeting. It's a blatant "I'm better than you" attitude, and it's rude.

I look at my calendar and planner every evening to prepare for the next day. I think about the clothes I'm going to wear and make sure they are clean and ironed, I ensure I have fuel in my truck or plan for enough time in the morning to get fuel, and plan for what I need to do in between my scheduled events. There's no excuse to be consistently late. You don't want to leave the impression that you are a poor planner and unorganized.

RESPECTFUL

Showing respect to everyone that you encounter on a daily basis is a good way to earn the respect of others. Think about the golden rule: treat others how you want to be treated. It sounds easy, and it is, but it is amazing how many people don't do this. Practice empathy. Treat everyone equally, it doesn't matter if it's the janitor, a coworker, your boss, or the CEO, everyone is important. Being a leader means that you expect people to follow in your footsteps. So, disrespecting people is telling others that that behavior is ok. Respect is hard to earn and easy to lose. Don't do things that will jeopardize your hard work and progress. Practice being a good person, and this will come back to you in so many ways.

PROFESSIONALISM

We've already somewhat discussed how important being professional is, but I want to take a minute to reiterate and drive home the message. When you are in a leadership role, people are watching. People are watching you to learn how to behave in situations. The last thing you want is someone watching you and learning how NOT to act in situations. Being professional, punctual, and respectful are things that everyone should be doing in your organization.

Dress professionally every day. Don't dress for the job you have now, dress for the job or level you are striving to achieve. Be the best dressed in your office. Take pride in the way you look and carry yourself. Be proud. That's the reputation you want. When your name comes up in a conversation, and you are not around to hear, what do you want people to say about you? You won't gain everyone's approval, ever, but by no means give anyone the opportunity to say that you aren't professional, respectful, and prepared every day.

ETHICAL

One of the most important aspects of being a good leader is being an ethical person. Your personal ethics should be your moral compass and should guide your actions day in and day out. Leaders should have a strong ethical moral compass and be bound to high standards of honesty, fairness, and legality.

Making unethical decisions not only makes you look bad but can also hurt a company's reputation and may have some legal ramifications that could cost the company a lot of money and time to overcome. As a leader, you will undoubtedly be put into situations where you are challenged with making a decision that could impact others in or out of your workplace. It's important to weigh those consequences and ensure you are making ethical decisions. And just because a decision may be legal doesn't mean it is ethical, fair, or the right thing to do. If you are ever unsure of a decision, I strongly suggest you reach out to someone who is certain that your decision is ethical and within legal boundaries such as Human Resources or your Legal Department. It's better to double-check than to put yourself and your company in a bad situation.

> Ethics definition - *Moral principles that govern a person's behavior or the conducting of an activity.*

SOFT SKILLS - CLOSING

Soft skills are the basic fundamentals that every good leader should have. These skills can always be improved upon and adjusted for different situations. Although most of these should be common sense, they are some of the most important traits people forget about when trying to accelerate their careers. You may have several degrees and years of experience under your belt, but if you aren't professional and come across as disrespectful, I will take someone with less experience than you every day of the week. Learn to communicate correctly, make ethical decisions, and be professional, it will pay off. Not only should you be honing your soft skills, but you should also be helping your team members hone theirs as well. Offer them training, role-playing exercises, or "what would you do" situational questions. Keeping your team polished and constantly improving their soft skills is always good. Remember, your team is a direct reflection of your leadership abilities.

Soft Skills - Work Page

1 Are you a good communicator?

   Yes: _____   No: _____

2 Do you listen when others speak and do not interrupt them?

   Yes: _____   No: _____

3 Does your team communicate effectively?

   Yes: _____   No: _____

4 Do your team members treat each other with respect?

   Yes: _____   No: _____

5 How will you help your team better their soft skills?

6 Do you know any managers or supervisors that are unprofessional?

   Yes: _____   No: _____

7 What makes them unprofessional?

Yes:_____   No:_____

8 Do you consider yourself to be professional (punctual, dressed properly, respectful)?

Yes:_____   No:_____

9 What are some things that you currently do that could be improved upon?

25

DIVERSITY

We hear the term *diversity* a lot. But what is diversity? Diversity refers to the many different or diverse types of people, including gender, race, nationality, religion, and age. Diversifying your workforce can bring various ideas, innovation, and creativity to your organization. Diverse groups have been proven to have a greater range of perspectives and can generate more high-quality solutions than less diverse groups. Having people from different parts of the world with different backgrounds can bring unique viewpoints to the table. Diversity increases constructive group processes and is positively associated with performance. Diversity is also associated with increased sales revenue, more significant market share, more customers, and greater profits. Bringing different people together in a team environment and creating a safe place for them to give opinions and suggestions creates positive work experiences with optimum results.

> Diverstiy inspires creativity ...

In my experience, the most diverse place I ever worked was overseas in the Middle East for a Government Contractor supporting military efforts. There were people from all over the world working towards the same goals. There were language barriers and cultural differences, but it created a very unique and inspiring atmosphere. The ideas shared from experiences from around the world brought so much more to the conversations we were having that it inspired new thought processes and solutions that I am certain we wouldn't have thought of on our own. It was enlightening, to say the least. I look back at that group of people and the things we accomplished, and I'm still astounded. Such a great experience. It would have been a shame if those individuals were not allowed to participate in those discussions. We would have missed out on a lot of great opportunities.

All employees should feel included in their workplace and be given equal opportunities throughout the employee lifecycle. Employees, regardless of age, gender, or race, should be respected and treated the same. Training, education, and promotional opportunities should also be available to all employees equally.

Things such as prejudice and discrimination do happen, but it is up to the leaders of the organization to set a positive example that is inclusive of everyone. Any negative act toward any person or group of people should not be tolerated. The best way to deal with any issues regarding prejudice or discrimination is to report it through the company's Human Resource department.

Don't let negative people hold you back. If confronted with any negative situation, whether it's discriminatory or any other issue, rise above it, report it, and keep working towards your goals. You are better than that, and these types of situations will only deter you from reaching your desired levels of success. Be kind and treat others as you want them to treat you. Lead by example!

Diversity - Work Page

1 Describe diversity in your own words?

2 Does your current place of employment have a diverse workforce?

Yes: _____   No: _____

3 Have you ever had to deal with discrimination or prejudice at work? If so, how did you deal with it?

Yes: _____   No: _____

4 If you noticed a coworker being discriminated against, how would you handle it?

26

BUILDING YOUR TEAM

Are you a department manager? A corporate executive? A business owner? Or someone looking to move into a leadership role? No matter your level, no matter your industry, no matter your goals, you will need a solid team to reach your true potential. Every "great" knows how to surround themselves with great team members. You cannot become great by yourself. You need people who share your vision and your passion. You need people you can trust. You need people with expertise in areas you may not be experienced in. But how do you find those team members? How do you keep them motivated and productive? Let's break this down into a few different categories.

THE INTERVIEW

When you are looking to add new team members by posting

open jobs or promoting from within, there are several factors you should consider before making those decisions. Ensuring the person you are considering will mesh well with your already established team is extremely important. You don't want someone coming in causing conflict or disruption within your group. You need to make sure their goals and vision align with your and your team's goals and vision. A good attitude is a lot of times more important than actual skills and experience. You can always teach the tasks associated with the job, but it is difficult to change a negative person with a bad attitude.

Be sure when interviewing candidates that you share your expectations of them and what you expect of your team. They need to understand what they are possibly getting into because they may realize that they aren't a good fit and make that decision for you. The last thing you want is to hire someone and surprise them on their first day of work with job expectations that aren't compatible with their experience, knowledge, or goals.

Ask those tough questions and let them talk. You will learn more about someone if you do a lot of listening. Ask them for examples of things they are proud of and aren't so proud of. The goal of an interview is to learn as much as possible about that person as you can. I may refer to a resume, but I typically don't even look at it when interviewing. I'm more interested in getting into an open dialogue with the individual and learning about their personality and if I think their attitude will fit into our culture. Their resume is what earned them the actual interview. The interview is an opportunity for you to get to learn about their personality.

Depending on the job being interviewed for, letting the other leaders on your team participate in the interview process can be beneficial. Especially if they are the ones that will have to work more closely with this individual, let them give you feedback. This doesn't mean they will make the final decision, but it's good to have an extra set of ears present during this process in case they pick up on something you may have missed. This may not work in every situation, but if there is an opportunity to get your team involved in the interview process, I recommend doing it. I've been in situations where my team members have picked up on crucial details that I completely missed. And if it wasn't for that information, I may have hired the wrong person.

Be sure to ask them if they have any questions for you. This is important. I am always impressed (sarcasm) by those who don't have any questions for the company representative interviewing them. Did the interviewer cover everything? Do they not care about the working conditions, the hours, the pay, the insurance, time off, advancement opportunities, etc? I doubt it. Which means they just want a job and aren't particular in the situation they are getting into. Those people tend not to stay around long and probably won't be a good fit.

When I look for new team members, I want to be sure they will add value to my team. Even if I am promoting or moving someone from within the company, I must ensure they will fit well with my group. Just because they may be good in another department or in a different capacity, doesn't mean they will be as productive on my team. When you do have open positions within your team or organization, this is a great time to bring in someone who will take you to the next level. I want someone who is energetic, a self-starter, motivated to succeed, experienced, educated, respectful, professional and makes me better. I look for people who will add value to my organization, that will create revenue for my business, make me look good, and inspire my other team members. Yes, these people do exist! Just take your time and choose wisely!

Remember, your team represents YOU!

GETTING TO KNOW YOUR TEAM

Getting to know your team and what makes each person tick is key. Every single one of us has certain things that motivate us. Some of us are money-driven, some of us like to be recognized, and some of us desire the need to feel wanted or appreciated. Each of us is different. Getting to know your team's individuality and what motivates them takes time and a lot of observation.

Take time out of your week to spend one-on-one time with your team members, especially your leaders. Depending on how big your team is, this shouldn't be hard to fit into your schedule, and it is important. For your team to be truly successful and stay at a high level of motivation, they need to have certain needs met. If your team feels underappreciated, not compensated fairly, or unimportant, they will start to slack, be less productive, and eventually look for somewhere else to work. Find out what makes your people happy. If you aren't doing this now, this is something that can be implemented right away with immediate results. This is extremely important for your day-to-day business to be consistently successful.

For those team members who like to be recognized, send out an email every now and then and mention their hard work and dedication, or give them praise in a group meeting. For those who are driven by money or promotions, sit down with them and go over the plan to get them to their next level. Make sure they understand that you recognize their efforts and that there is more in the near future. There is nothing wrong with an employee who wants more, as long as they are willing to put in the work and have a good attitude.

Know their strengths and their weaknesses. Help them overcome their barriers and obstacles. Being a leader means you must guide them. To guide them effectively, they must be motivated. For them to be motivated, you must know what motivates them. Know your team.

ENSURE YOUR TEAM MEMBERS KNOW YOUR PRODUCT OR SERVICE

Now that you've gotten your team together and figured out how to keep them motivated, it's time to ensure they know your product and/or service that you or your company is providing. Even if your team is a support group such as Human Resources or Accounting, they will be more beneficial to your company if they understand the business they are involved in. I've seen so many people over the years who had no idea what the company they worked for did. Even though they were part of a group that did not perform the work or sell the product, it still seemed awkward that they couldn't discuss what the company they worked for did for money.

Be sure you include all employees on new product releases, new services, updates, and changes within the company. This is something that I have noticed over the years that a lot of companies disregard. Everyone must know the product or service you are providing.

Test your employees on things they should know. Make them describe what services or products you provide in their words. This is a good way to ensure they absolutely get it. Ask a different employee each week to describe one of the products or services to your entire team. Keep them on their toes and keep everyone involved. This will be a learning experience for both you and your team.

It's also good to cross-train employees in different roles within different departments when the situation allows. This can't be done for every circumstance, but it is good for those who can do so. This will give those employees a better understanding of what others are going through day-to-day. It may even help them develop a better process to help support those other departments. The more your employees understand the products, services, processes, and procedures, the better off your company will be.

CRITICAL FEEDBACK

No matter what kind of business you are in or the size of

your company, giving and receiving feedback professionally is very important. "Bad" feedback is just as important, or even more so, than good feedback. You need to know when there is room for improvement. The same goes for you being a leader giving feedback to your team.

I make a habit of getting with my direct reports and give them critical feedback at least once a month. I don't wait for an end-of-the-year review. Consistent feedback, good or bad, is better and more frequent. If someone is doing well, they need to know that. Everyone likes a pat on the back for a job well done. This will reinforce those good habits, and it will also keep those employees motivated by them knowing you are paying attention and appreciating their efforts.

When an employee needs work in a particular area, that feedback is also critical. How would they know they need to improve if you are not letting them know? Good, positive, constructive feedback with a plan for improvement is a necessity, and they will appreciate it, if not now, then definitely in the future.

> *"We all need people who will give us feedback. That's how we improve."*
>
> Bill Gates

Remember, when praising your employees, it is perfectly okay, and even better sometimes, to do it in public. That means a lot to people when you single them out in a good way to praise them. But never give negative feedback or discuss areas for improvement with an employee in front of everyone else. Those conversations need to be held behind closed doors in a one-on-one environment. There is no need to embarrass or humiliate anyone for making a mistake. They will appreciate the advice and respect you more for doing it in a professional manner.

Whether the feedback is good or bad, it is needed. I've been in situations where I've witnessed other leaders in organizations frustrated at one of their employees to the point of termination and in one instance, demotion, without giving them any feedback at all. After a conversation with both individuals, I asked them if they had given those employees any feedback or clear expectations on how to improve their performance. Both said no. In both situations, both leaders thought the employees should have known that their performance was poor. That shocked me. I couldn't understand how a leader in an organization could be so frustrated at one of their employees and never have a conversation with that employee regarding their performance. Both situations were unacceptable, in my opinion. I would never let it get to that point without having multiple conversations with those employees and a plan for improvement.

Your employees will appreciate good honest feedback. Meet with them regularly. Keep emotions out of the conversation. Stick to the facts and always discuss a plan moving forward.

You should also be willing to accept feedback without reacting in a negative way. We never stop learning and evolving as people, so there will always be room for improvement. Feedback is necessary even for us. Feedback is a gift. Welcome it with open arms.

CONFLICT RESOLUTION

There will undoubtedly be times when you have disagreements with those on your team and possibly with those who you may report to. But there is a difference between a simple disagreement and escalating it into an actual fight. Arguments can sometimes be healthy, but when it becomes personal and escalates beyond a disagreement, they can leave long-term, negative lasting effects.

Being part of a team, whether you are leading the team or a crucial team member, you will be surrounded by people day in and day out with different personalities, from different age groups, with different attitudes, from different backgrounds, and that are dealing with different problems outside of the workplace. It is important to remember that everyone is an individual and on their own life path. Treat everyone with respect because you never know what they are dealing with at home or outside of the workplace.

There will be times when you can try as hard as you can to avoid conflict, but conflict will still find you. A good pointer on being the bigger person and not taking the bait from a negative coworker or even a boss is first, don't react. Before you say anything, walk away.

If you walk away and don't give that person the reaction they want or expect, you've already won. This will give time for the moment to calm, give time for you to think before reacting wrongly, and it makes you immediately look like the more mature, professional person.

Another tip is not to take what others say personally. Sometimes people are just having a bad day. Sometimes those people immediately regret what they say. And sometimes you may just be taking it wrong, and those people didn't mean to be negative or mean towards you at all. Once again, walk away. Take time to breathe and think.

Some other tips for workplace conflict with others in your group, your boss, or employees who report to you are:

- Put your emotions in check; stay professional
- Respect other people's opinions even if you think they are wrong
- Listen carefully to others; give them time to speak
- Keep an open mind; you may find out they are right
- Look for common ground and be willing to compromise
- Take responsibility if you are wrong; apologize if necessary
- Don't insult others; keep the conversation professional
- Avoid absolute statements such as "you are always", or "you never"
- Focus on the issues, nothing personal
- Keep the promises you make; follow through

By following these simple steps, you will be able to resolve most issues at work. Unfortunately, there may be times where no matter what you do, you won't be able to avoid the problem. At that time, you must notify the necessary people to help resolve the conflict, either your supervisor, Human Resources, or Employee Relations. No matter what, stay calm, and don't get on their level. You are meant for greater things other than workplace drama and are on the path to success. Don't take the bait, you will thank me later.

Building Your Team / Conflict Resolution - Work Page

1 When choosing a new team member, what is the most important characteristic you look for?

2 Is it Important that new team members get along with others on your team?

Yes: _____   No: _____

3 Who does your team represent?

4 Do your team members completely understand your business and what your company provides?

Yes: _____   No: _____

5 What can you do when dealing with a negative person who creates conflict at work? How do you avoid that negativity?

6 When you get to work tomorrow, how will you motivate your team to be their best?

7 Is getting to know what motivates your team members important?

Yes:_____   No:_____

8 What should be your initial reaction when confronted with a negative person with an aggressive attitude?

27

THE IMPORTANCE OF CULTURE

Think about your current workplace. Think about the employees' attitudes and work ethic that make up your organization. How would you describe it if someone asked you? Are the employees happy? Do they enjoy coming to work? How does your team interact with each other? Your company culture starts from the top of the organization and should trickle down to every individual within the company. Suppose your culture isn't defined and properly communicated from the top-level leadership. In that case, it probably isn't the culture the company is striving for or at least the culture that could benefit your company to the maximum extent possible.

Company culture, also referred to as organizational culture or corporate culture, is defined as a shared set of values, goals, attitudes, and practices that make up an organization. The first step is for those values and goals to be identified. How would you describe your current culture and the culture of your leadership team? Do you have goals and values identified? How are you communicating those goals to your employees? Are they reiterated and reinforced throughout the year? How are you keeping your employees motivated to reach those goals? Are you holding your team members accountable? What kind of culture are you trying to build? What makes your company a great place to work, and what sets you apart from your competitors? What kind of behaviors are valued at your company, and what are your company values?

These are questions you should be asking yourself and the leaders of your organization. Together, you should come up with a set of values, and live and breathe those values each day. Remember, as a leader, your employees and team members look at you to learn how to behave and act. If you are straying from these set values, they will likely stray as well. You need to have total buy-in from your team, especially your leaders.

Your company values should not only be in a mission statement or an email to your employees but also in your handbook, work practices, policies, and procedures. Your workforce should be aligned with these visions, with a clarity of the company's purpose and values. And for this culture to truly transpire there will need to be reinforcement throughout the year and a system to hold each employee accountable.

The 4-step process to create a successful company culture:

1. Define your company culture -
   a. What is the purpose, the mission, and values of your organization and/or team?
2. Organizational adoption of culture –
   a. Ensure your values are reflected in your handbook, policies, procedures, and work practices. Leaders at all levels need to drive this.
3. Create awareness throughout your organization –
   a. Meetings, events, emails, signs, and any other form of communication.
4. Sustainability –
   a. Reinforcement and accountability with each employee. Ensure your leadership is driving the culture and leading by example.

Since most of us spend a good chunk of our lives (about a third of our day on average) at work, our workplace environment should resemble and align with our own personal beliefs and attitudes as much as possible for us to be as productive as possible. This alignment will also help the organization's retention rate. When employees are happy and feel appreciated, they will stay longer. When there is a disconnect between the company's culture and the employees, higher attrition will happen, and more unproductive employees will stay longer; both scenarios are unhealthy and expensive for the organization.

If you take the same employee, and move him/her from a

bad, unorganized, unidentified culture, to a more structured, nurtured, defined culture with total buy-in from the employees that work there, do you think that same employee would work the same in both situations? No. That employee will be more inspired, motivated, and much more productive in the defined healthy culture. That employee will stay longer, work harder, and be more beneficial to the company. And when employees are loyal, they spread that positive energy to other employees. It will impact your business on so many different levels. If you take care of your culture and your employees, they will take care of your business and your customers.

Company culture and the company's core values are essential. But living them, being an example, and enforcing them throughout the organization is even more important. Define your culture but enforce the follow-through. Your company culture will carry you to the next level, or will keep you stagnant or even be your ultimate demise. Culture takes time to develop, but consistent, persistent enforcement of those values and goals is the key to its success.

Culture - Work Page

1 What are your current company values and goals?

2 Describe the culture at your workplace?

3 Does your leadership team have complete buy-in regarding your company values and goals?

Yes: _____   No: _____

4 Do you communicate your company values and goals to your teams and other stakeholders in your organization?

Yes: _____   No: _____

5 Do you think your company culture aligns with your work practices?

Yes: _____   No: _____

6 Are your company values included and reflected in your handbook, policies, and procedures?

Yes: ____   No: ____

28

WHAT IS PROGRESS?

You've heard me say progress equals success throughout this book. The definition of progress is *moving forward toward a destination*. The destination for you will be different than anybody else's. Your goals will be different from mine, and the way you get to your goals will be unique as well. Figuring out your end destination is the part you need to work on first. Be honest with yourself. What is your big ultimate goal? Where do you want to be in 10 years?

When choosing your destination, make sure that it will make you happy once you've reached it. Make sure you will have to push yourself hard to reach that goal. Don't make it easy. Ask yourself, should you be setting your destination further down the road? Make your destination something you would be proud of. After you've determined your ultimate goal, then the rest is just hard work and details. Every day, you should be inching closer and closer to that destination.

Progress is like drops of water into a bucket. It doesn't seem like much in the beginning, but after a few days it starts puddling, then rising, and eventually it will reach the top. Every day, you should look at your daily planner and make an intentional effort to be closer than you were yesterday. You will have to reflect a lot and be honest with yourself about your progress. Have you reached a dead-end? Do you need to work on a skills gap that will help you get to the next level? Continue to invest in yourself and be self-aware. You will know your obstacles better than anyone else.

<u>Be addicted to your progress</u>. Nothing will get in your way because you are on a mission. Daily progress equals success.

You are here X ___ Progress ___ Destination X

"Progress lies not in enhancing what is, but in advancing toward what will be."

Khalil Gibran

29

BECOME A MENTOR

This is my favorite section. One of the best feelings I get from doing what I do, is being able to pass on my knowledge and experience to others who are on their way to achieving their goals and dreams. I've had several different mentors throughout the years, and I would not be in the position I am in today without them. If someone is willing to learn and put in the effort of being better than they were yesterday, I am more than willing to do my part in sharing helpful tips and lessons I've learned throughout my career.

As I've mentioned before, I've watched, observed, listened to, and talked with, so many different people throughout the last 20 years that it is impossible for me to count. But a few have taken the time to give me some good advice along the way. I've had some extremely helpful people who have taught me things such as patience, anger control, consistency, and how to lead with confidence.

One of my favorite mentors was a man named Jerry Kieffer. I met him in Baghdad, Iraq in 2004 when we both worked for a government contractor. I had already been on that project for several months when he was brought in from another project.

At first, I observed. We didn't know each other, so that is all I could do. But as time passed and we worked together more, we built a better relationship. I appreciated the way he led and organized our teams. I was young and hadn't been around many seasoned leaders at that point. I had big responsibilities at that time, and a lot of people were relying on me to make good and fast decisions. And I relied on Jerry for guidance. He helped me come up with resolutions for difficult situations, and we would brainstorm different outcomes and discuss various strategies. This helped me think methodically and in a different way than I was used to.

I gained a tremendous amount of confidence working for and working with Jerry, and I'm not sure I would have had the career I had without him being there with me at that moment in time. So, I am very thankful for the time he spent mentoring me throughout those couple of years. Because of him, I have done this with several people since then throughout my career.

It's important to me to give back. It makes me feel accomplished. That's why I enjoy writing material such as this book and developing training programs. I enjoy speaking to kids in my community and teaching them about opportunities that exist. I like to get involved with nonprofits and talk with families and young adults to try to motivate them and guide them with some positive direction. I've taken several young adults and given them opportunities to work for me, and even if they leave my organization I still keep in touch and give them advice. I feel like it's my duty to pass on my information to whoever is willing to listen. So many people have helped me throughout my life, it is the right thing for me to do.

Pass on your information. Mentor someone or several people. Teach others what you've learned, the bad and the good. Give them advice, guidance, and support. This will make you feel good, and it is always fun to watch those you've helped along the way succeed.

Remember those who have helped you, and be sure to thank them as you reach your goals.

Mentor - Work Page

1. Do you have a current mentor?

   Yes: _____   No: _____

2. Do you mentor anyone?

   Yes: _____   No: _____

3. In your opinion, what makes a person a great mentor?

30

FINAL THOUGHTS

Being a good leader is the key to a successful career. Constantly improving your leadership skills and investing time and resources on self-progression should be one of your highest priorities. As you go through your career and start to pick up your own techniques and ways of leading your teams, you will start getting more comfortable making those tough decisions that your team and organization rely on. Always improving is the goal. With steady progress it is easier to stay motivated and inspired to want more. Want more for you. Want more for your "why". Expect more from yourself. Forget about settling and compromising. We get one shot at this life, make the best of it. You don't want to leave this world without anyone knowing you were here.

> You don't want to leave this world without anyone knowing you were here ...

One of my dad's favorite poems was *The Dash Poem* by Linda Ellis. It's often read at funerals, and I read it at my dad's memorial service. But I think it is essential to understand the meaning behind this poem while you still have time to make a change.

The Dash Poem
By Linda Ellis

I read of a man who stood to speak at the funeral of a friend. He referred to the dates on the tombstone from the beginning to the end.

He noted first came the date of the birth and spoke the following date with tears. But he said what mattered most of all was the dash between the years.

For that dash represents all the time that they spent life on Earth. And now only those who loved them know what that little line is worth.

For it matters not how much we own, the cars, the house, the cash. What matters is how we live and love, and how we spend our dash.

So, think about this long and hard. Are there things you'd like to change? For you never know how much time is left that can still be rearranged.
If we could just slow down enough to consider what's true and real, and always try to understand the way other people feel.

Be less quick to anger and show appreciation more, and love the people in our lives like we've never loved before.
If we treat each other with respect and more often wear a smile, remembering that this special dash might only last a little while.

So, when your eulogy is being read with your life's actions to rehash, would you be proud of the things they say about how you spent your dash?

Everyone has that dash. Whether you are 20 years old, 40 years old, or 100 years old. It's not the amount of time that dash represents, but what was accomplished and the differences you made in other people's lives. You want people to remember you for being a good person, a hard-working person, a successful person, a leader, a mentor, and someone who took care of their "why". Since you get to read this book and poem, there is still time to make adjustments. The only time it is too late is when this poem is being read at your funeral.

Your success is ultimately up to you. If you read this book but don't commit to the processes or implement any changes, then it will be just as beneficial as buying a gym membership and never going to the gym but expecting to lose weight or gain strength. You will only be as successful as the amount of energy and effort you put into it.

Being a leader is something you should be proud of. It is an important role no matter what level of leader you currently are. Take what you've read in this book and implement it into your daily lives. You will absolutely see positive results. You may already do some of the things we discussed in this book, but that shouldn't deter you from doing them better or more.

Being a good leader is something you should continually work on every day. Remember, success takes time, so be patient. As long as you are putting in the work, planning your days, making good choices, and inching closer to your goals each day, you will become the leader and obtain the success that you desire. Be addicted to progress and your commitment to your own success.

When things are slow in your life, or you feel stagnant in your career, this is the perfect time to hone your leadership skills. You want to be prepared when opportunities present themselves. They will undoubtedly present themselves, and it is up to you to be ready to pounce. Stay curious, take calculated risks, and don't set limitations on your abilities.

FINAL THOUGHTS

Now that you've gone through this book and you are determined to succeed, it's time to put some action into play. There is no magic pill to succeeding, it takes working hard, learning, taking risks, networking, and consistency.

Here are three simple rules that you should remember and follow:

1. If you don't go after what you want, you'll never have it.
2. If you don't ask, the answer is always no.
3. If you don't step forward, you're always in the same place.

As for me, I am going to continue to learn and work on myself. I will continue to inch closer to my big goals. I won't let people or other obstacles stand in my way. And I hope you do the same!

Thank you for reading this book and going on this journey with me!

Be addicted to your progress!

GLOSSARY

Accountability - the fact or condition of being accountable; responsibility.

Anxious – experiencing worry, unease, or nervousness, typically about an imminent event or something with an uncertain outcome.

Average – compromising or settling instead of progressing towards something great.

Barriers – An obstacle that most people will see as a reason not to succeed, but not you! You will run right through them!

Choices – an act of selecting or making a decision when faced with two or more possibilities.

Company Culture – a set of shared values, goals, attitudes and practices that characterize an organization. It's important to note that company culture is a naturally occurring phenomenon; your team will develop a culture whether intentionally or not.

Comparison – a consideration or estimate of the similarities or dissimilarities between two things or people.

Complacency – Settling for less! Giving up!

Completer – Someone who finishes what they start.

Compromising – is commonly understood as giving up something in order to reach a place of understanding with your partner. In this book, we refer to compromising with oneself.

Conflict – a serious disagreement or argument, typically a protracted one.

Consistency – Doing the right thing over and over and over to ensure positive results!

Decisions – the action or process of deciding something or of resolving a question.

Decisiveness – the ability to make decisions quickly and effectively.

Discrimination - the unjust or prejudicial treatment of different categories of people, especially on the grounds of ethnicity, age, sex, or disability.

Diversity – the practice or quality of including or involving people from a range of different social and ethnic backgrounds and of different genders, sexual orientations, religions, etc.

Dreams – a cherished aspiration, ambition, or ideal.

Education – Anything that you read, watch, or attend, that makes you better!

Effort – strenuous physical or mental exertions.

Empathy – the ability to understand and share the feelings of another.

Employee Attrition – is the departure of employees from the organization for any reason (voluntary or involuntary), including resignation, termination, death or retirement.

Employee Retention – the ability of an organization to retain its employees and ensure sustainability.

Ethics – moral principles that govern a person's behavior or the conducting of an activity.

Expectations – a strong belief that something will happen or be the case in the future.

Feedback - information about reactions to a product, a person's performance of a task, etc. which is used as a basis for improvement.

Franchise – an authorization granted by a government or company to an individual or group enabling them to carry out specified commercial activities, e.g., providing a broadcasting service or acting as an agent for a company's products.

Garbage – a thing that is considered worthless or meaningless.

Human Resources – a department that manages the employee life cycle. This includes recruiting, hiring, onboarding, training, performance management, administering benefits, compensation and firing.

Hungry – having a strong desire or craving. In this book, we are referencing a hunger for success, progress, happiness, and goal completion.

Initiative – an act or strategy intended to resolve a difficulty or improve a situation; a fresh approach to something.

Intentional – On purpose, with purpose!

Interpretation – the action of explaining the meaning of something.

Journey – an act of traveling from one place to another.

Kurt Lewin – was a German-American psychologist, known as one of the modern pioneers of social, organizational, and applied psychology in the United States.

Leader – You! Someone who can influence and motivate a team or group to achieve a common goal!

"Let them" – People are going to talk when you start working hard and progressing. There is no need to respond. Just "let them".

Limitations – Limitations are something that limits a quality, achievement, condition, or activity.

Locus of Control – Locus of control refers to the degree to which an individual feels a sense of agency in regard to his or her life.

Mentor – Pass on information that you have learned to others who are trying to reach their goals!

MGC – Make Good Choices! All the time!

Negativity - the expression of criticism of or pessimism about something.

Networking – the action or process of interacting with others to exchange information and develop professional or social contacts.

Peter Principle – the principle that members of a hierarchy are promoted until they reach the level at which they are no longer competent.

Positivity – the practice of being or tendency to be positive or optimistic in attitude.

Practice - repeated exercise in or performance of an activity or skill so as to acquire or maintain proficiency in it.

Prejudice – preconceived opinion that is not based on reason or actual experience.

Progress – Forward movement toward a destination.

Public Speaking – an organized, face-to-face, prepared, intentional (purposeful) attempt to inform, entertain, or persuade a group of people (usually five or more) through words, physical delivery, and (at times) visual or audio aids. In almost all cases, the speaker is the focus of attention for a specific amount of time.

Realistic – having or showing a sensible and practical idea of what can be achieved or expected.

GLOSSARY

Relentless Progression – Making no excuses for yourself! Amid chaos and confusion, you are still focused and determined to succeed! Nothing stands in your way!

Satisfied – contented; pleased.

Self-Awareness - conscious knowledge of one's own character, feelings, motives, and desires.

Soft Skills – The fundamentals that every individual should have on your team! These can always be improved upon and should be reinforced constantly throughout your work week.

Sole Proprietorship – also referred to as a sole trader or a proprietorship—is an unincorporated business that has just one owner who pays personal income tax on profits earned from the business.

Success – Being better than you were yesterday! Steady Progress!

Team – A group of like-minded individuals that work together to achieve greatness!

The Dash Poem – "The Dash,", written by Linda Ellis, at its core, is a narrative poem. It follows the story of a man speaking at the funeral of a friend. As he gives a eulogy, he shares that the dates on the headstone don't really matter at all. What's really important is the "dash" between the birthdate and the death date.

Timeline – a chronological arrangement of events in the order of their occurrence.

Variation – a change or difference in condition, amount, or level, typically with certain limits.

Addicted to Progress / Successful Leadership

A₂P